UNSOLVED

DEATHS

METRO BOOKS
New York

An Imprint of Sterling Publishing Co., Inc.
1166 Avenue of the Americas
New York, NY 10036

ISBN 978-1-4351-6928-9

For information about custom editions, special sales, and premium
and corporate purchases, please contact Sterling Special Sales
at 800-805-5489 or specialsales@sterlingpublishing.com.

Manufactured in Singapore

2 4 6 8 10 9 7 5 3

sterlingpublishing.com

Design: JC Lanaway
Photo Credits: see page 224

UNSOLVED

DEATHS

STRANGE DEATHS AND MYSTERIOUS DISAPPEARANCES

CHARLES PHILLIPS

METRO BOOKS
New York

CONTENTS

INTRODUCTION

Death grips our attention powerfully. We puzzle over why we die, what the experience of dying might be like, and what, if anything, happens to us after death. We ponder the matter of when we will die ourselves, and we tend to be fascinated by the details of others' deaths: What brought the victims to their end? What was their final act? Were they tricked, murdered, assassinated, or did they rush headlong to their own extinction? Were they the victims of natural forces, of accident? The past is rich in cases of unsolved deaths that fascinate endlessly because there is no clear answer to one or more of these questions. Forty of these such cases, featuring great historical figures as well as leading lights of the modern world, are the subject of this book.

Some deaths are unsolved because the victim is missing. We start with these, in "The Disappeared," traveling from Nefertiti, the supremely elegant consort of Pharaoh Akhenaten in Ancient Egypt, to 1970s Chicano activist Oscar Zeta Acosta, best known as the character "Dr. Gonzo" in Hunter S. Thompson's wild and celebrated novel *Fear and Loathing in Las Vegas*. In these cases, and others that also feature, some people have doubted whether the principal character in the story did in fact die at its end. We may like to imagine that these people who ducked out of the historical narrative somehow cheated death—they lived on, at least in the stories of possible sightings.

Other cases of unsolved death are more like a traditional detective story. We have the body, we know the victim was killed, but we cannot determine who did the dastardly deed. In surveying cases of this type, our second chapter, "Killers Unknown," covers one of the most famous unsolved murders in British history: the beating to death of Julia, wife of Liverpool insurance salesman William Wallace, on January 20, 1931. This case may in fact be the much searched-for "perfect murder."

Then—covered in "Accident, Suicide—or Murder?"—there are deaths that, while they look like they occurred by chance or were suicides, may have been premeditated killings. This chapter ranges

Above: There is no doubt that King William II died on his horse, but was it an accident or an assassination?

over 900 years, from King William II of Norman England, reputedly killed in a hunting accident that may have been an assassination in 1100, to the death of Australian astrophysicist Rodney Marks, whose death by poisoning in 2000 is claimed by some as the first murder at the South Pole.

With some deaths—covered in "Conspiracy Killings?"—the lack of clarity about the death has led to colorful explanations in the form of conspiracy theories. The death of King Edward II of England in 1327 is notorious for its gruesomeness, but some think an official cover-up allowed Edward to live out his life in Europe.

The final category, "They Were All Lost... Group Tragedies," covers the cases of lost army units, groups of travelers, and crews of explorers. Famous examples include the wiping from history of the famous Roman Legio IX Hispana and the disappearance of Ludwig Leichhardt, intrepid explorer of the Australian Outback.

However hard historians, amateur sleuths, and curious readers puzzle over the incomplete evidence, they are unable to reach a definitive verdict and are dependent on new facts emerging that will solve the case. This book is an unmissable guide to these intriguing unsolved deaths, complete with a regular feature, "Strange Stories," that details some of the more outlandish theories that attempt to explain such dramatic mysteries.

THE DISAPPEARED

The lives of many great historical figures have ended in mystery. We cannot be sure how these celebrated women and men died because their final movements are unknown and their bodies could not be found. Their fame means that colorful stories and counter-stories have developed over the years about their last days and their unsolved death. Australian premier Harold Holt seemingly drowned in the surf off Cheviot Beach in Victoria in 1967, but there are claims he was killed by the CIA, abducted by aliens, or was a Chinese spy, taken by submarine to China. In some cases, we know where a person died but not how or why. French aviator and author Antoine de Saint-Exupéry crashed in the Mediterranean in 1944 while flying in World War II, but did he lose control or was he shot down by the Luftwaffe? His aircraft was found but his body never identified.

The lack of clarity around such deaths has led to claims that the supposed deceased in fact lived on, in disguise or under another name. Did the Ancient Egyptian Queen Nefertiti disappear because she took the throne and ruled as a man? American outlaws Butch Cassidy and the Sundance Kid supposedly died in a shootout in 1908 after being tracked down in Bolivia, but did they escape and live out their lives in obscurity, as some eyewitnesses claim? Conspiracy theories and reported sightings have cast doubt over the certainty of some famous deaths, allowing the legends, at least, to live on.

Left: This film still of the notorious outlaw duo Cassidy and Sundance shows the shootout, but what happened afterward?

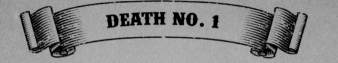
WHAT BECAME OF NEFERTITI?

Date: ca. 1330 BCE
Location: Egypt

Partway through her husband's reign, Nefertiti, revered wife of Pharaoh Akhenaten, suddenly disappeared from public life. Did she die of plague or was she murdered by jealous priests?

Nefertiti was the beautiful Queen of Akhenaten, Pharaoh of Ancient Egypt in the fourteenth century BCE. She was a famed beauty and even her name translates to "the beautiful one has come." She ruled alongside her husband at a time of great change, when Akhenaten attempted to sweep away the traditional Ancient Egyptian religion, with its pantheon of gods and goddesses, and introduce a new faith based on the worship of a single god—the sun god Aton.

In Ancient Egypt, pharaohs often had more than one wife. Nefertiti, who may have been a princess of the Mitanni from Syria but was probably the daughter of a leading courtier named Ay, was selected to marry the future Akhenaten at the age of 15, ca. 1355 BCE. Over the next decade, the couple had six daughters.

Above: The now-ruined ancient city of Akhetaton was built especially as part of Akhenaten and Nefertiti's religious dedication to the sun god Aton.

Nefertiti may also have been the mother of the boy-king Tutankhamun, probably the most famous of all Ancient Egyptian pharaohs, whose lavish tomb, filled with treasures, was discovered in 1922 in the Valley of the Kings near Thebes—a burial ground for several dynasties.

THE NEW RELIGION

Akhenaten and Nefertiti's religious revolution may have made enemies of the priests of Ancient Egypt. The pharaoh originally ruled under the name Amenhotep IV, but took a new name that means "of benefit to Aton." He moved his capital from Thebes to a new site alongside the river Nile. Here he built a vast city called Akhetaton—now known as Tell el-Amarna—centered on a huge temple dedicated to Aton. Akhenaten demanded that images of Amon, revered as king of the gods, be removed from temples. New religious images showed Akhenaten, Nefertiti, and their children receiving the blessings of Aton, who is represented as the disk of the sun. The pharaoh and the queen were the focus of Aton's blessings and were themselves revered as semidivine beings.

Nefertiti was Akhenaten's principal consort and chief wife, and the pair ruled alongside each other at the head of the state and the new religion—an Ancient Egyptian power couple. Nefertiti, her husband, and the sun god formed a kind of divine trinity, and the queen was worshipped as a fertility goddess. Some carvings show her in the guise of a pharaoh, making offerings, humiliating Egypt's enemies, and riding in a chariot.

Below: In 1912 a bust of the queen by the sculptor Thutmose was discovered by archaeologists in the ruins of Akhetaton and placed on display in Berlin. This slender-faced beauty has since become one of the most celebrated icons of Ancient Egypt.

VANISHED OR BANISHED?

In the twelfth year of Akhenaten's reign, ca. 1341 BCE, the king's daughter Meketaten died and Nefertiti disappeared from public life. At one time historians thought she was somehow disgraced and had to retire to live on in relative obscurity in the north palace at Akhetaton or in Thebes, but this theory is now thought to be wrong. Some believe she perished in a plague that swept the city ca. 1341 BCE; others say she may have been killed by priests ousted and sidelined by the new religion of Aton that she and her husband promoted.

At the end of Akhenaten's reign, the old religion of Amon was revived. The new city of Akhetaton was abandoned and the capital moved to Memphis. The old temples were restored. Was Nefertiti eliminated as part of this counterrevolution?

MISSING BODY

Nefertiti's body has never been found. If she died before the abandonment of Tell el-Amarna, then she would have been buried there. Evidence exists that one or more royal burials from Amarna were reinterred in the Valley of the Kings, but still no mummified remains that could be identified as Nefertiti have been unearthed.

— STRANGE —
STORIES

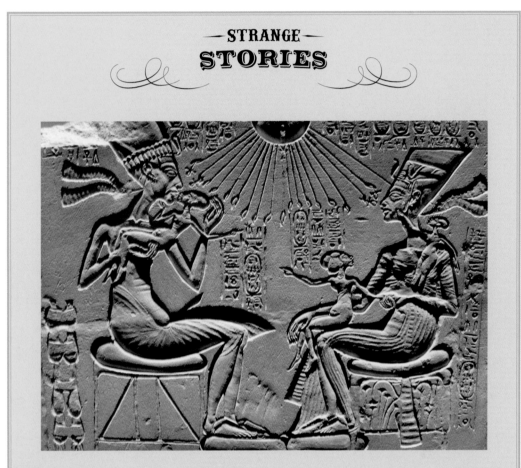

Some historians believe that Nefertiti's name disappeared from the public record because she ruled in male guise as a pharaoh. They argue that the male ruler with the coronation name Ankhkheperure and personal name Neferneferuaten, who appears to have ruled alongside Akhenaten toward the end of his reign, was in fact Nefertiti under another moniker. Then, after

Above: This sunken relief depicts Akhenaten, Nefertiti, and three of their daughters.

Akhenaten's death, she perhaps ruled alone as pharaoh under the name Smenkhkare before, in 1333 BCE, the throne passed to the boy-king Tutankhamun, who may have been her son.

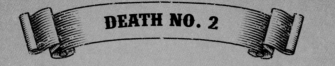

WHAT HAPPENED TO THE LAST BYZANTINE EMPEROR?

Date: April 1453
Location: Constantinople (modern-day Istanbul, Turkey)

Emperor Constantine XI Palaeologus disappeared in the sacking of Constantinople by the Turks in 1453. Did he go down fighting, flee, or was he—as legend has it—rescued by an angel?

As his invading Ottoman army prepared to besiege the great city of Constantinople, capital of the Byzantine Empire, Sultan Mehmed II offered Byzantine Emperor Constantine XI a way out. Surrender the city and his life would be spared, and he could even continue to rule in a reduced capacity, in Mystras, Greece. Constantine was defiant: "It is beyond my authority to surrender the city. We who live in it will freely die in its defense."

Constantine was putting his life on the line to defend the remnants of the Byzantine Empire, once the eastern half of the mighty Roman Empire. It had endured for more than 1,000 years after the collapse of the Western Roman Empire in the fifth century.

Constantinople had been founded by Roman Emperor Constantine the Great, as a "new Rome," in 330 CE, on the site of the Ancient Greek trading colony, Byzantium.

Born in 1404, Constantine XI had come to the imperial throne in January 1449 after the death of his brother John VIII. He would prove to be the last in a long line of Byzantine emperors stretching all the way back to Constantine the Great, who died in 337 CE.

FACING THE OTTOMAN THREAT

Constantinople had long looked vulnerable to the rising power of the Ottoman Turks, who emerged in Anatolia from ca. 1300 onward. Ottoman sultan Murad II attempted to besiege the city in 1422 but failed. Then, in April 1453, Mehmed II imposed a new siege.

Below: This statue of the brave warrior Constantine XI Palaeologos stands in Athens, Greece.

To prevent supplies and relief troops getting in from the sea, Mehmed blockaded the waters of the Bosporus, the 17-mile (31-kilometer) strait that links the Black Sea and the Sea of Marmara. He built a powerful fortress, the Rumelihisari, at the narrowest point of the strait. Mehmed's army also had powerful cannons that could—and did—breach the formidable city walls of Constantinople. The Golden Horn— the part of the Bosporus that leads into the city—was protected by a defensive chain in the water designed to prevent ships passing, but Mehmed managed to haul his fleet overland.

Nothing could stop the Ottoman advance, and 55 grueling days of siege only weakened the resolve of the city's defenders. At last, on May 29, 1453, the Ottomans launched their assault. Constantine led the Byzantine soldiers in their attempts to halt the tide of attackers, who surged into the city after

breaching the Circus Gate. The last known sighting of the Last Byzantine Emperor was near the Gate of Saint Romanus, as he fought with his sword alongside his troops.

THE BITTER END

There are various accounts of what happened next, none verified. One is that Constantine was caught in the fighting, beheaded, and the head given as a trophy to Sultan Mehmed II. However, surely the Sultan would have made much of this—perhaps displaying the head—and, as a result, we would know of it. Another theory is that he tried to flee by boat but was caught and beheaded by Turkish troops. A third account is that, overcome by fear, Constantine asked a comrade to kill him but before this could happen he was trampled in the fighting and his body lost. Another version claims that Constantine did manage to get away and was still alive more than 10 years later. We do know that the city was a riot of looting and slaughter for three days before Mehmed was able to restore order. It is not surprising that the Emperor's body was lost—particularly because he had thrown off all marks of his rank and so was dressed as an ordinary soldier. His corpse was likely buried in a mass grave or left to rot in the streets.

Above: Mehmed's fortress, the Rumelihisari, still stands strong today, after almost 600 years.

Right: Does the Golden Gate of the ancient Walls of Constantinople house a hidden chamber that contains the Emperor's body, delivered there by an angel?

— STRANGE —
STORIES

The strangest of all the theories about what happened to Constantine is the legend that as the Turks poured into the city on the day Constantinople fell, an angel saved him from harm. His fate was not to live on in sorrow: the angel turned the Emperor into marble and placed him in a hidden chamber near the city's Golden Gate. There he sleeps and waits for the day appointed by destiny when he will be roused and lead a Christian army to take back what is now Istanbul and make it a Christian city once more. In this he is like other fallen leaders, such as King Arthur in Britain, who reputedly will awake from the sleep of centuries to right wrongs and restore freedom. The legend of Constantine's rescue became popular in the 1820s during the Greek War of Independence against the Ottoman Empire.

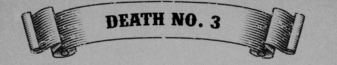

HOW DID THE TERRIFYING VLAD THE IMPALER MEET HIS END?

Date: December 1476
Location: Wallachia, Romania

Count Dracula's namesake, a devilish fifteenth-century prince in what is now Romania, may have been killed in a military skirmish in 1476—but his body was never found.

Vladislav III, Prince of Wallachia, became known as Vlad the Impaler (in Romanian, Vlad Țepeș) from the gruesome humiliation he inflicted on his enemies when he impaled their bodies on stakes—supposedly putting 100,000 people to death in this terrifying way. He is also known as Dracula, meaning son of Dracul. His father had taken the name Dracul ("Dragon") when he joined the knightly Order of the Dragon, founded by the Holy Roman Emperor Sigismund to fight the Ottoman Empire.

Wallachia was a dangerous place—at the boundary between the Muslim Ottoman Empire and Christian Europe. And Vlad knew all about the Ottomans. For six years after his father had become prince in Wallachia in 1442, he and his brother Radu were held prisoner at court by the Ottoman Sultan Murad II, to ensure their father's good behavior. Vlad left and returned home in 1448, the year after his father had been assassinated by unruly boyars (local noblemen).

For eight years after that, Vlad fought for control of the principality, briefly taking power in 1448 but being ousted, and finally winning out in 1456. One account tells how he invited the boyars who had risen against his father to dinner, seemingly extending the hand of forgiveness and fellowship, but then had his troops murder them—and mounted their mangled bodies on stakes as a final insult.

Above: This woodcut depicts Vlad callously sitting down to his dinner alongside his impaled victims. Wonder what was on the menu...

FOLK HERO

Three years earlier, Constantinople had fallen to the Ottomans (see page 14). For his tireless campaigns against the Turks, Vlad became celebrated as a folk hero. In these years, he consolidated his fearsome reputation as "The Impaler." Famously, in 1462 he left thousands of victims impaled on a battlefield to deter Ottoman troops from pursuing him. On another occasion he reputedly spiked a group of Ottomans in a different way: the story goes that he had a meeting with envoys from the Ottoman sultan to discuss a peace settlement and asked them to remove their turbans as a mark of respect; when they refused, he had his men nail the turbans to their heads, so that they need never take them off again.

The life and byname of Vlad the Impaler seem to have been inspirations to Bram Stoker, Irish author of the vampire classic *Dracula* in 1897. A whole series of novels, radio and stage plays,

TV shows, and classic movies sprang from Stoker's Gothic novel about a count from Transylvania (in Romania) who bites his victims in the neck to draw their lifeblood, which, as a member of the undead, the count needs to drink to survive. Stoker read about the horrific Vlad the Impaler in a book called *An Account of the Principalities of Wallachia and Moldavia*, by British diplomat William Wilkinson, and reputedly told his son Irving that he had a terrifying dream afterward. It inspired a deathless classic.

DEFEAT—AND DEATH?

In December 1476 Vlad was defeated in a skirmish somewhere between Giurgiu and Bucharest with an army led by rival Prince Basarab Laiotă, who had Ottoman backing. According to one version of what happened next, supplied by an ambassador to Buda from Milan, the victorious Ottomans sliced Vlad's body into pieces. Another account comes from Antonio Bonfini, an Italian humanist–historian at the court of King Matthias Corvinus in Hungary, who said the prince's head was sent as a trophy to Mehmed II—the same fate, according to some, that befell defeated Byzantine Emperor Constantine XI (see page 16).

Below: A statue of Vlad keeps watch over the citadel of Sighişoara, where he was born.

Some say Vlad's remains were buried in the Snagov monastery, Budapest, but in the 1930s archaeological investigations found that the site said to be his grave contained the remains of horses. Another theory was that he was buried in a monastery-fortress, near the battlefield where he supposedly died. Whatever became of him, he achieved immortality through his namesake Count Dracula.

— STRANGE —
STORIES

A new theory emerged in 2014 about what happened to Vlad after the 1476 skirmish. Scholars from Tallinn University, Estonia, argued that he was taken prisoner and hauled off in chains by the Ottomans, destined for imprisonment or a grisly execution; but then he was ransomed by his daughter Maria, who was living in Italy. The scholars propose that Vlad is buried in the genteel surroundings of Santa Maria La Nova Church in Naples. A tomb there, in the same churchyard as his daughter's grave, is decorated with a dragon (suggesting Dracula) and two sphinxes, which are said to be a reference to Thebes, also called Ţepeş.

Above: The tomb in Santa Maria La Nova Church is effectively "signed" with the fearsome count's name: Dracula Ţepeş.

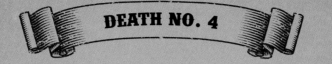

WHERE DID SUPER-PIRATE HENRY EVERY END UP?

Date: 1696

Location: Last seen in New Providence, Bahamas

Henry Every, also known as "Long Ben," led a stunning pirate raid on Indian Mughal Empire ships—then, with the price of £1,000 on his head, disappeared. Was he killed, or did he die a peaceful death back home in the English West Country?

One of the most notorious pirates of the seventeenth century, Henry Every was a veteran of the Royal Navy who led a mutiny onboard the *Charles II* at Corunna, Spain, on May 7, 1694, renamed the warship the *Fancy*, and embarked on a life of piracy. He had already taken rich pickings from ships around Africa when in 1695 he took command of a hastily assembled pirate squadron that sailed to the mouth of the Red Sea to pounce on a fleet of Mughal ships, returning from Mecca in Saudi Arabia, with *Hajj* pilgrims and treasures aboard.

Every chased and engaged the *Ganj-i-Sawai*, a dhow, and its escort vessel, the *Fateh Muhammed*. The pirates' cannonballs broke the mainmast of the dhow and the men boarded the two ships, engaging in a fierce hand-to-hand struggle. It was the stuff of the devout passengers' worst nightmares—people were raped, killed, and even, supposedly, stabbed themselves or leaped overboard to escape the pirate terror. Several pirates were themselves killed in three hours of brutal hand-to-hand fighting, but Every emerged unscathed from the skirmish with no less than £600,000 worth of jewels and coins—a staggering haul equivalent to more than $65 million today. At a stroke, he became the world's richest buccaneer.

THE WORLD'S FIRST MANHUNT?

In response, the East India Company and the Privy Council in London announced a bounty of £1,000 on Every's head. So began what is believed to be history's first global manhunt, but the pursuers did not get their man— Every disappeared.

The *Fancy* and its fleet anchored off the island of New Providence in the Bahamas, known as a refuge for pirates, and—after negotiations with the island's governor, Sir Nicholas Trott, which included a huge bribe—the pirates were allowed to come ashore in the capital, Nassau. When news arrived of the warrant for Every's arrest, Sir Nicholas had to tell the authorities where the pirates were—but he warned the outlaws first.

They fled in all directions, some to North America, some back to Europe, and, while 24 of the men involved were eventually caught, and six were hanged for their crimes in London in 1696, Every himself got away. Did he change his name and succeed in hiding out somewhere in the tropics? One account has him sailing homeward with some of his men aboard the *Sea Flower*, which was bound for Ireland, where he came ashore and went to ground.

Above: The notorious English pirate and his ship, the *Fancy*, capture a treasure ship of the Mughal Empire in the Red Sea.

RULER OF A PIRATE KINGDOM?

Every became a hero for a generation of pirates, including the famous Edward Teach, known as "Blackbeard," and John Rackham, known as "Calico Jack," and many probably fictional accounts of his later life were soon circulating. One of these tells how, in the raiding of the *Ganj-i-Sawai*, he encountered and was smitten by the Mughal emperor's daughter; they later married and, after escaping his pursuers, Every settled on Île Sainte-Marie, off the coast of Madagascar, where he presided over a pirate kingdom, commanding an army of 40 ships and 15,000 men, and even minting his own gold coins. Although the pirate realm on Île Sainte-Marie was probably invented by the author Adrian van Broeck, who first described it in a book in 1709, its existence was very widely accepted and people even claimed to be diplomats sent to the courts of Europe on the pirate king's behalf.

Some sources say that to strike fear into the hearts of rivals and victims, Every flew a black flag with a white skull above a pair of crossed bones on the *Fancy*—if he did, he was the first pirate to do so. The sources say that the skull on Every's flag—shown in profile—wore an earring and a bandana. Other authors claim he flew a red flag decorated with four chevrons, thought to be an attempt to link him to the celebrated Avery or Every family, members of the British aristocracy who had four chevrons on their coat of arms.

Every was celebrated by author Daniel Defoe in two of his books and by Charles Johnson in his play *The Successful Pyrate*, first performed in 1712. This king of pirates achieved immortality in literature and popular history, and is still celebrated today.

Below: Was the idyllic-looking Sainte-Marie Island, Madagascar, home to a pirate realm?

— STRANGE —
STORIES

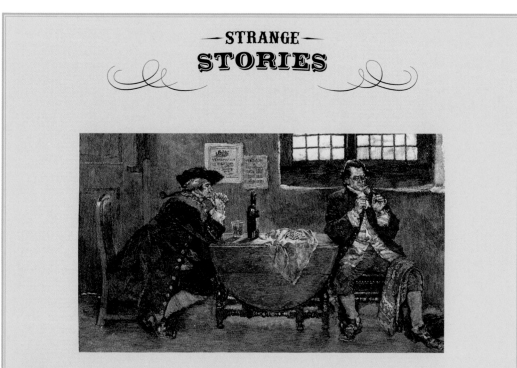

Above: Henry Every consults a merchant in Bristol about a set of plundered Indian jewels. His broker then showed himself to be equally crooked, making off with the loot.

Was one of the world's greatest robbers the victim of a scam? One report suggests that after going to ground Every made his way home and settled in the West Country, where he changed his name and lived peacefully into old age. If this is true, he must have enjoyed the stories circulating about him and his life as pirate king on Île Sainte-Marie, and his flying of the "Jolly Roger" flag, and it must have taken supreme self-discipline not to boast of his exploits to those he met. Some say his plans for a quiet old age ran aground when he was cheated and robbed.

He tried to sell his haul of jewels on the quiet, but he was swindled by merchants in Bristol—and reduced to abject poverty. John Knill, mayor and customs collector in St. Ives, Cornwall, was later told by one of Every's descendants that the former pirate had suffered in poverty in his last years and been buried as a pauper in Barnstaple, Devon.

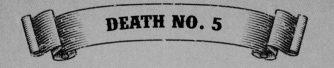

WERE BUTCH CASSIDY AND THE SUNDANCE KID NAILED IN THAT FINAL SHOOTOUT?

Date: November 7, 1908
Location: San Vicente, Bolivia

Wild West outlaws Butch Cassidy and the Sundance Kid were famously killed in a shootout near San Vicente, Bolivia, in the early hours of November 7, 1908. Or were they?

Butch Cassidy and the Sundance Kid—real names Robert LeRoy Parker and Harry Longabaugh—fled to South America in 1901 when lawmen threatened to catch up with them in the US. Members of the notorious Wild Bunch, they robbed trains and banks across the western US through the 1880s and 1890s. Their lives and their supposed end were immortalized in the iconic 1969 movie *Butch Cassidy and the Sundance Kid*, directed by George Roy Hill and starring Paul Newman as Butch, Robert Redford as Sundance, and Katharine Ross as Sundance's girlfriend Etta Place, and with a celebrated Burt Bacharach score.

Above: A wild bunch indeed. Sitting (left to right): Harry A. Longabaugh, alias the Sundance Kid; Ben Kilpatrick, alias the Tall Texan; Robert LeRoy Parker, alias Butch Cassidy. Standing: Will Carver, alias News Carver; Harvey Logan, alias Kid Curry.

Robert LeRoy Parker embarked on life as an outlaw in around 1884 and took his name from his mentor Mike Cassidy. After a couple of years as a cowboy and two in Wyoming Prison from 1894 to 1896, he teamed up with Harry Longabaugh. Longabaugh took his name from the town of Sundance, Wyoming, where he was imprisoned for the only time in 1887, aged 17, after stealing a horse. Among the Wild Bunch outlaws he was reckoned to be the fastest and best shot.

GOING WILD

The story goes that during 1896 and 1897, Butch Cassidy called together around 200 outlaws to a meeting at Brown's Hole, a valley near the point where the Utah, Colorado, and Wyoming borders meet. He proposed setting up a syndicate of train robbers, which became known as the Wild Bunch. Butch did not, in fact, become the leader, because after contesting this position with Kid Curry—real name Harvey Logan—he gave way.

Above: A worn, grammatically flawed sign welcomes visitors to San Vicente, Bolivia, the final resting place of Butch Cassidy and the Sundance Kid...or is it?

The Wild Bunch worked in small groups, robbing trains and banks, rustling cattle, and stealing horses. They were the most successful bank-robbing crew in the West.

ON THE RUN

Sundance, Etta Place, and Butch escaped Pinkerton detectives by fleeing to New York City in 1901 and then moved on to Argentina, where the three tried to go straight and run a ranch for four years. In 1906 they embarked on a fresh crime spree—robbing mines, trains, and banks in Argentina, Chile, Peru, and Bolivia. In 1907 Sundance helped Etta, who was unwell, return to the US, then went back to his partner in crime in Bolivia.

The official story is that the pair were cornered by Bolivian cavalry and died in a shootout in a boarding house near the mining town of San Vicente, Bolivia. Two American outlaws had robbed an agent of a mine and seized the payroll money, around 15,000 pesos. The owner of a boarding house became suspicious, alerted the authorities, and Bolivian police and soldiers surrounded the building. During the ensuing gunfight one soldier was killed and one injured; then later one of the men inside was heard screaming in pain. A shot was heard in the house and the screaming ceased; then a second shot rang out, and all was quiet.

On entering the house, the police found two bodies and surmised that one of the bandits had been fatally injured and his partner had killed him to end his agony before taking his own life. The locals identified the two men as the robbers of the payroll, but did not succeed in proving they were Butch Cassidy and the Sundance Kid. The corpses were buried in the local cemetery. Experts have since attempted—without success—to find physical remains that could be identified as those of the outlaws.

— STRANGE —
STORIES

As a result of there being a lack of identified remains, the final fate of the two outlaws is a mystery. One account claims they were killed when a bank robbery went wrong in Mercedes, Uruguay, in 1911. Others report that they managed to go underground and return to the US. Some say Butch made a living in Mexico and the US, notably Alaska, until the 1930s, and that he died in 1937, possibly in Johnnie, Nevada, or Spokane, Washington. Several people claim he was seen in Baggs, Wyoming, a former stamping ground of the Wild Bunch, driving a Ford Model T car, in 1924.

Meanwhile, some people claim that the Kid lived on under the name Harry Long, perhaps in Casper, Wyoming, and survived until the 1930s or even, in one version, to 1957.

Below: Was it really Butch who was spotted in 1924 driving a Ford Model T car?

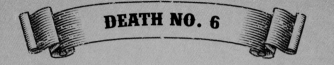

HOW FAR DID MALLORY AND IRVINE CLIMB?

Date: June 8, 1924
Location: North Face of Mount Everest, Tibet

George Mallory and Andrew Irvine went missing while attempting to climb to the summit of Mount Everest in 1924. What disaster befell these intrepid mountaineers?

George Mallory was an English gentleman—University of Cambridge graduate-turned-schoolmaster, veteran of World War I, and a member of the exalted Alpine Club for climbers. He and Guy Bullock, a friend since their time together at the elite Winchester College, mapped out a probable route to the 29,029-foot (8,848-meter) summit of Everest, the world's highest mountain, during the Alpine Club's first major trip to the mountain in 1921. Mallory was the climber who, when asked why people wanted to climb Everest, famously replied, "Because it's there." He took part also in the Alpine Club's second expedition, in 1922, when they reached an altitude of 27,300 feet (8,320 meters) but then had to turn back, and a further attempt was ended by an avalanche that left seven porters dead.

Mallory went missing with Andrew Irvine during the Alpine Club's third attempt to conquer the mountain the following year. He and Irvine set out on June 6 for their assault on the summit. The conditions were not particularly favorable, with winds and snow hampering the climbers. On the morning of June 8, they left their final camp at a height of 26,800 feet (8,170 meters), with two bottles of oxygen each. Later that day, one of the other expedition members looked up when mists briefly cleared and glimpsed the two Englishmen. That was the last time they were ever seen.

Below: Mallory (left) with Irvine, in the last known photo of the pioneering pair on their fatal Everest climb in June 1924.

Right: Whether they made it to the top or not, the explorers were hailed as heroes in the press, and beyond.

FINDING MALLORY

Various finds over the ensuing years have helped interested experts piece together a little of what occurred. Still today, though, we do not really know what happened and, crucially, whether the two men ever reached the summit.

The major discovery came in 1999, when Mallory's body was found at 26,768 feet (8,159 meters). He had clearly suffered a major fall; there was a hole the size of a golf ball in his forehead, which might suggest his ice axe bounced off a rock and hit him on the head, killing him. With his body, explorers found his pocketknife with its leather slipcase, some letters, a pair of snow goggles, and his brass altimeter, but not what they hoped for above all—the camera they believed would hold clues as to whether he had reached the summit.

Many years earlier, in the 1930s, Irvine's ice axe had been found at a height of 27,700 feet (8,440 meters). Also, some climbers claimed to have seen Irvine's body, but it has never been found. A Chinese mountaineer, Wang Hungbao, said in 1979 that four years earlier he had seen what he called an "English dead" at

26,575 feet (8,100 meters). He said the body was face up and had a hole in its cheek. The very next day, Wang died in an avalanche, and as a result was not able to show others exactly where the body supposedly lay. Another climber, Xu Jing, said in 2001 that he had seen Irvine's body 41 years earlier (in 1960). Supposedly it was lying with its feet pointing toward the summit, its face visible and black from the effects of frostbite. He gave two possible locations, at heights of 27,230 feet (8,300 meters) and 28,050 feet (8,550 meters), but searches in the places he indicated did not turn up the body.

There are many theories about what happened. One is that, with Irvine suffering from exhaustion, Mallory took his oxygen bottles and made a solo ascent to the summit. Another is that both attempted the summit but had to turn back due to exhaustion. It seems that they were tied together by rope for safety as they descended, but one slipped and pulled the other off. Both fell to their deaths.

Below: Mallory's preserved body was found on Mount Everest in May 1999, but his camera is still missing.

THE FIRST TO SUMMIT?

The men credited with being the first to climb Mount Everest are Edmund Hillary and Tenzing Norgay, who achieved the feat on May 29, 1953. It is quite possible that they were beaten to it by Mallory and Irvine almost 12 years earlier—only, these two climbers did not live to tell the tale. As we have seen, there are many theories about what happened on that fateful day. Two pieces of evidence suggest that they fell when descending, after having climbed to the summit. First, Mallory apparently carried with him a photo of his wife that he was determined to leave on the summit; when his body was found, although there were many well-preserved papers, there was no photo—suggesting he had left it on the summit. Second, Mallory's snow goggles were in his pocket, indicating that he was not wearing them when he fell, perhaps because the pair were heading back down after dark, having climbed to the summit—and conquered the mountain.

Below: Mallory and Irvine's 1924 route had to tackle the north face of the mountain, as the southern side was off-limits, accessible only through Nepal, which was, at the time, a forbidden kingdom to foreigners.

SUMMIT

Second step
First step

Camp 6
26,800 feet

Northeast
Ridge

Great Couloir

Camp 5
25,196 feet

Camp 4
22,965 feet

Mallory's
body found

— STRANGE —
STORIES

Mallory was known to be a climber of almost superhuman ability. A story told by poet and novelist Robert Graves in his book *Goodbye to All That* celebrates an incident that occurred in 1908 on Mount Snowdon in North Wales, when, halfway down one of the Liwedd precipices on the mountain, Mallory turned back to retrieve his pipe, which he had left on a ledge. The following day, colleagues from the Climbers' Club, the elite of rock climbing in England and Wales, examined the route he had taken and found it was an overhang the entire way—by normal standards impossible to climb. Afterward, the club named the climb "Mallory's Pipe, a variation on route 2" and said it was "totally impossible," but added, "it has been performed once, in failing light, by Mr. G. H. L. Mallory." The anecdote suggests Mallory definitely had the ability to top Everest, and in all likelihood reached the summit in 1924, before he fell victim to a terrible accident on the way back down.

Above: Mallory's pipe was made famous by the remarkable climb he made to retrieve it on Mount Snowdon, Wales, in 1908.

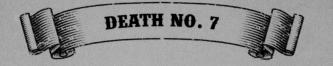

WAS PERCY FAWCETT KILLED WHILE SEEKING THE LOST CITY OF Z?

Date: May 29, 1925
Location: Mato Grosso, Brazil

British explorer Percy Fawcett, friend of authors H. Rider Haggard and Arthur Conan Doyle, disappeared in Brazil. Did he die of natural causes or was he killed by local tribes?

Percy Fawcett was an Edwardian gentleman-explorer, a decorated World War I veteran, army major, and experienced trekker. According to some sources he may have been the inspiration for the character Indiana Jones. After he disappeared on his last trek in search of what he called the "Lost City of Z," on May 29, 1925, several expeditions attempted to follow in his footsteps and find out what had happened to him, but his unsolved death remains shrouded in mystery.

Fawcett completed a surveying mission for the Royal Geographic Society in 1906 on the borders of Brazil and Bolivia and returned to the area seven times between 1906 and 1924. By 1914 he had developed his theory of the City of Z, in the Mato Grosso region of western Brazil, which he believed was the chief base of a great civilization that had once existed in the Amazon River basin. He had found remains of delicate pottery and was convinced that beneath the jungle floor was evidence of roadways and great causeways. (Recent finds by anthropologist Michael Heckenberger and others suggest that Fawcett may have been right: there is evidence of a city and large civilization, home to around 60,000 people, of ca. 800–1600 CE in roughly the area where Fawcett was looking; it is named Kuhikugu, after the main archaeological site.)

Fawcett was searching for Z in 1914 when World War I broke out. Despite being almost 50 years old, he insisted on returning to fight and took command of an artillery brigade. He was promoted to lieutenant colonel and awarded a Distinguished Service Order (DSO), but by 1921 he was back in the jungle, making a solo attempt to find Z. This time he fell sick with fever and ended up having to shoot his sickly horse at the place he later called "Dead Horse Camp."

Above: A real-life Indiana Jones, Fawcett was known for his daring expeditions to the Amazon.

FINAL ATTEMPT

Fawcett returned once more in 1925 with his son Jack and Jack's best friend, Raleigh Rimell. They had substantial backing from London financiers and were well supplied with powdered milk, canned food, flares, guns, and navigational instruments. In the party were two locals, two dogs, two horses, and a pack of eight mules.

The group departed from Cuiabá, capital of Mato Grosso, on April 20 and made good progress. The last communication, sent to Fawcett's wife, Nina, and dated May 29, from Dead Horse Camp, said he was about to go on across the Upper Xingu River with Jack and Raleigh. He wrote to Nina, "You need have no fear of failure."

Above: Was the Upper Xingu River in Brazil the famous explorer's final destination?

When they were not heard from again, people wondered if they had starved to death, been killed and eaten by wild beasts—or if they were alive and living among the natives. This last explanation was given weight by Swiss explorer Stefan Rattin, who claimed that on October 16, 1931, he met Fawcett, who was being held captive by tribesmen near the Tapajós River in northwest Mato Grosso. The following year Rattin set off with two men, one a reporter, to rescue Fawcett, but was never heard from again.

The majority assumed Fawcett, Jack, and Raleigh had been killed by local tribes. Most subsequent expeditions either turned up no evidence or found clues to suggest they had died at the hand of Indian tribes.

Below: The oral legends of the Kalapalo describe their historic encounters, and suggest that the tribe did come across Fawcett and may have been the last to see his expedition alive.

KILLED BY THE KALAPALO?

Danish explorer Arne Falk-Rønne reported that he learned what had happened to Fawcett from Orlando Villas-Bôas, a Brazilian activist in support of the rights of indigenous Amazon tribes, who

lived among the locals and said he had met one of the tribesmen who had killed the explorer. The story was that the explorers had traveled with gifts for the local Indians, as Fawcett knew this was required to guarantee a good reception, but an accident on the river meant they lost all the gifts. The Kalapalo tribe decided to kill the three explorers rather than allow them to go on to a possibly much more violent end at the hands of aggressive tribes ahead. Falk-Rønne said a tribesman confirmed this story.

Above: Expedition leader Villas-Bôas shows what he believes to be the skull of Fawcett to reporters in the town of Xavantina, Brazil, in 1951.

In the 1950s Villas-Bôas claimed he had been given Fawcett's bones by a tribesman, but analysis proved they were not genuine. In 1998 British explorer Benedict Allen visited the Kalapalo Indians and their chief said that his people had nothing to do with Fawcett's disappearance. In 2005 American writer David Grann also visited the Kalapalo and was told a new version of events. According to this, the three explorers had stayed with the Kalapalo before heading eastward, despite warnings that the Indians in that direction were very fierce and would likely kill the intruders. The Kalapalo said they saw the smoke from the explorers' campfire for five days, but then it did not show any more. They were convinced that Fawcett, Jack, and Raleigh had been killed by the tribesmen.

— STRANGE —
STORIES

Is it possible Fawcett never intended to return to England, determined to set up a commune in the jungle? This is the explanation of Fawcett's final trip proposed by TV and theater director Misha Williams, based on Fawcett family papers that had previously been kept secret. Williams said Fawcett had visions of a native goddess or spirit who drew him to the area, and that many friends had agreed to follow him there once he had created the community, which was to follow a strange new religion based on Theosophy (an esoteric philosophical-religious tradition influenced by Hinduism and Eastern religions and believing in reincarnation) and the worship of Fawcett's own son, Jack. Williams wrote a play, *AmaZonia*, about the affair. What's more, the major Hollywood movie *The Lost City of Z* leans toward suggesting Fawcett and Jack were carried off to their end by native cannibals, but leaves room for viewers to decide whether the intrepid Brits died or lived on in the jungle.

Right: Fawcett (Charlie Hunnam) and his son Jack (Tom Holland) are surrounded by Amazonians in the 2017 movie *The Lost City of Z*.

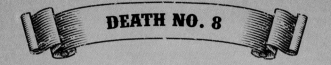

WHAT BECAME OF THE BARONESS OF THE GALAPAGOS?

Date: March 27, 1934
Location: Galápagos Islands, Pacific Ocean

Evidence suggests that sexual jealousy among 1930s pioneers on the Galápagos Islands was once sufficiently rife to spark a violent murder.

The self-styled Baroness Eloise Wehrborn von Wagner Bosquet, a flamboyant and attractive Austrian, had come to the Galápagos from Paris in 1932, with her two German lovers, Philippson and Lorenz, to try their hand at pioneer living—reputedly with plans to establish a grand hotel as a stopping-off point for wealthy American yacht owners. The trio had been attracted by press coverage of the hardy pioneer life of German doctor Friedrich Ritter and his lover and former patient Dore Strauch, who had established a homestead on the rugged and unspoiled Floreana Island in 1929. Floreana is one of the Galápagos Islands, most famous for their connection to English naturalist Charles Darwin, pioneer of the theory of evolution, who visited in 1835 to study the islands' many endemic species.

BACK TO BASICS

Ritter and Strauch's life on Floreana became well known in Europe after the letters they sent home were published in the press. They were followed in 1931 by another German party—Heinz Wittmer, his pregnant wife Margret, and their teenage son. They and the Ritters largely kept apart but got along tolerably well. When the Baroness arrived with her two companions and a manservant, she certainly stirred things up— naming her homestead the "Hacienda Paradise," wearing a whip and carrying a pistol, and even calling herself "Queen of Floreana." Her reputation spread, and before long American yachtsmen were calling at the island specifically to see the now notorious Baroness—and get the material for a juicy anecdote with which to regale friends later on.

Above: The Baroness was an eye-catching woman who attracted attention—which was just what she intended.

The other residents began to suspect she was interfering with their mail and spreading malicious gossip about them. Her *ménage à trois* came under severe strain, with Philippson regularly beating Lorenz, who would flee to the safety of the Wittmers' house, but eventually always drag himself back to the Hacienda Paradise with his tail between his legs. Meanwhile, the relationship between Ritter and Strauch also deteriorated quite severely.

Then on March 27, 1934, the Baroness and Philippson suddenly disappeared. Margret Wittmer claimed that the Baroness had said she was departing with Philippson on a yacht passing through on the way to Tahiti. She said she was leaving the great bulk of her possessions to Lorenz; the pair never turned up on Tahiti. Not only that, but afterward, when people began to investigate, they realized that no yacht had come through at the time when the pair disappeared. No trace of their bodies was ever found.

THREE MORE DEATHS

This gruesome mystery was followed by three further untimely deaths. First, Lorenz decided to leave the island, and found a Norwegian fisherman by the name of Nuggerud to take him to Santa Cruz Island and thence to San Cristóbal Island, from where he would be able to catch a ferry to mainland Ecuador. These two men also came to a mysterious end. After they were seen in Santa Cruz, they disappeared. Their bodies were later discovered on Marchena Island, one of the northern Galápagos.

Then the original pioneer Friedrich Ritter died, just eight months later. The official reason was that he had severe food poisoning after eating some chicken, but people were doubtful of this explanation since he was a vegetarian and an experienced pioneer who would have known at once if meat had gone off.

These events have gripped historians, and were even the subject a movie, *The Galapagos Affair: Satan Came to Eden*. Officially, the Baroness and Philippson disappeared, while Ritter died in a case of accidental food poisoning; and no one knows how or why Lorenz and Nuggerud ended up on Marchena Island. The evidence prompts many to suspect wrongdoing, and the "Galapagos Affair" remains a troubling unsolved mystery.

Above: Lorenz's body is found on a beach, mummified and dried out, and accompanying the body of Nuggerud, the fisherman who tried to help him leave.

— STRANGE —
STORIES

Two of the key survivors of this carnage—Margret Wittmer and Dore Strauch—had their own theories about what really happened. Strauch believed that the Baroness and Philippson never made it off the island but were killed by the jealous and frequently humiliated Lorenz, and then the Wittmers, who had taken pity on him, helped him cover up the deed. Strauch thought that the bodies had been burned in an acacia wood fire, which gets hot enough to destroy skeletal

Above: Friedrich Ritter and his lover Dore Strauch established the Floreana homestead in 1929. Only one would survive to tell the tale.

evidence. Wittmer, however, always stuck to the official story that the pair had left the island by yacht—right up to her death in 2000. Meanwhile, she believed that Strauch had deliberately poisoned Dr. Ritter. She claimed he had cursed his former patient as he lay dying.

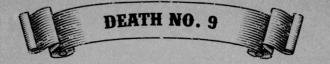
HOW DID AVIATRIX AMY JOHNSON DIE?

Date: January 5, 1941
Location: Thames Estuary, Kent, England

The pioneering British flier disappeared while delivering an RAF aircraft in World War II. Did she drown or was she fatally wounded by the propellers of a rescue boat? One theory suggests she was shot down by friendly fire.

By 1941, British airwoman Amy Johnson had a string of records to her name. She was the first woman to fly solo from the UK to Australia and had set speed records from Britain to India, Japan, and South Africa. The newspapers celebrated her as "Queen of the Air." In 1940, to support the war effort, she joined the Air Transport Auxiliary, whose role was to move RAF aircraft around the country to where they were needed. On January 5, 1941, she was delivering an Airspeed A.S.10 Oxford monoplane from Prestwick to Oxford, but went off course in terrible weather and disappeared over the Thames Estuary.

FLIGHT'S GOLDEN AGE

Like Antoine de Saint-Exupéry (see page 52) and celebrated American flier Amelia Earhart, Johnson belongs to aviation's romantic age. Fearless fliers of both sexes took their lives in their hands in pursuit of distance and time records, while their flights were followed by a hungry public through breathless press reports. The pilots were lionized for their daring, but it came at a price: all three of these, and many other aviation pioneers, lost their lives.

Johnson learned to fly while working as a secretary in London, and just two years later embarked on her triumphant solo flight from England to Australia in her de Havilland D.H.60 Gipsy Moth named *Jason*. In just under three weeks, May 5–24, 1930, she covered 11,000 miles (18,000 kilometers), from Croydon, near London, to Darwin in the Northern Territory of Australia.

Below: Amy Johnson— pictured here on her airplane prior to her attempt to break the England–Australia flight record—was a revered darling of the skies.

Above: Tumultuous crowds cheer Johnson (waving from the car) after her long-distance solo flight from London to Australia in 19 days.

The queen of the air found her king when she married another pilot, Jim Mollison, after he proposed to her mid-flight—and just eight hours after they met—in 1932. That year she set a solo record from London to Cape Town, and in 1933 she and Mollison flew to the US in a D.H.84 Dragon I, *Seafarer*. They didn't make it to their destination, Brooklyn, but crashed in Connecticut after running out of fuel. The pair were injured and needed time to recover, but were later given a ticker-tape parade on Wall Street. The records to India and South Africa followed in 1934 and 1936, but the airborne romance faded: Amy and Mollison divorced in 1938, and Amy reverted to her maiden name.

On January 5, 1941, Johnson took off in the Airspeed A.S.10 Oxford from Prestwick, Scotland, intending to fly via Blackpool to RAF Kidlington in Oxford, but—off course in a snowstorm—ran out of fuel and bailed out of the aircraft, which crashed into the Thames Estuary near Herne Bay in Kent.

CONFLICTING ACCOUNTS

Sailors on board HMS *Haslemere* saw Johnson land in the water, shouting for help. The traditional version of what happened next is that Lieutenant Commander Walter Fletcher dived in to try to save Johnson, but failed due to the rough sea and extreme cold. Johnson went missing and Fletcher lost his life in a hospital a few days later from his injuries and the effects of exposure to the conditions.

Below: Amy and her fellow pilot husband, Jim Mollison, agreed to marry eight hours after they met, but the marriage crash-landed in divorce only six years later.

-49-

Another version has recently been proposed. Historian Dr. Alec Gill wrote in 2016 that Johnson may have been caught up in the propellers of the boat that had come to her rescue after it went backward rather than forward. The new account is based on one received from a naval reservist who was serving on the *Haslemere*. According to this version, it was after this had happened that Fletcher dived in to try to save Johnson. The navy then covered up this terrible accident to save face. Other cover-up theories center on the contention that Johnson had a secret passenger on board, and that her flight was about more than simply moving a monoplane. Some people have claimed that more than one body was seen in the Thames Estuary after she bailed out. We will never know for sure what happened on that fateful night.

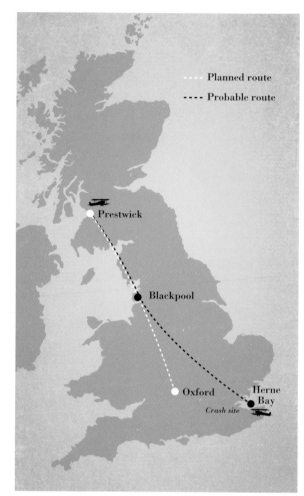

Johnson's body was never found, but it was evident that the queen of the air was dead. A memorial service was held in the beautiful central London church of St. Martin-in-the-Fields on January 14, 1941, and a British biopic, *They Flew Alone*, was made the following year, starring Anna Neagle as Johnson and Robert Newton as Jim Mollison. Johnson is commemorated at the RAF Memorial at Runnymede, near Windsor, southern England.

Above: Johnson's plane veered way off course in a snowstorm on what would prove to be her final flight.

Planned route
Probable route

Prestwick

Blackpool

Oxford

Herne Bay

Crash site

—STRANGE—
STORIES

Above: The British adoration for Amy lived on in this 2003 postal stamp, but was it British servicemen who ended her life?

Was Amy Johnson really a victim of friendly fire? A recent theory suggests she was shot down by British gunners in error. In 1999 Tom Mitchell, who was serving as a gunner at Iwade on the Thames Estuary on January 5, 1941, said he believed he and his fellow gunners downed Amy Johnson's aircraft by mistake. According to Mitchell, the gunners received orders to shoot down an unidentified plane, and after the pilot of the plane failed to give the correct identification code, fired 16 rounds of shells. Mitchell was serving with the 58th Heavy Anti-Aircraft Regiment of the Royal Air Force; in civilian life he was a gardener and he was 83 when in 1999 he reported what he believed had happened. He said the gunners had asked the pilot of the unidentified aircraft to cite the color of the day (an agreed code) and she had twice given the wrong answer. So they believed the aircraft was an enemy and fired the 16 shells that sent the plane crashing into the estuary— though they could not see that at the time in poor conditions. The next day they were devastated when they discovered that the famous Amy Johnson's aircraft had gone down at this time. Mitchell added that the gunners were instructed to keep quiet about what had happened. Another rival theory suggests Johnson was shot down in error by a British naval convoy.

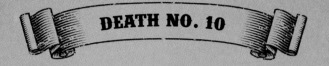

WAS *THE LITTLE PRINCE* AUTHOR SHOT DOWN BY THE LUFTWAFFE?

Date: July 31, 1944
Location: Mediterranean Sea, near Marseille, France

Antoine de Saint-Exupéry disappeared on a reconnaissance flight in 1944; in 2008 a former Luftwaffe pilot said he thinks he shot down the author-turned-military pilot.

French aviator and author Antoine de Saint-Exupéry is known above all for his lyrical novella *The Little Prince*, which has been translated into hundreds of languages and sold 150 million copies worldwide. He was flying for the Free French Air Force when he seemingly crashed into the Mediterranean Sea, near Marseille, on July 31, 1944. His body was never identified.

Saint-Exupéry was a hero of the romantic early years of aviation, when intrepid pilots defied the odds in fragile, wind-battered aircraft, with very basic navigational equipment. He survived several dramatic crashes, including one in 1935 in the Libyan desert that partly inspired the events described in *The Little Prince*. In the fable-like book, a pilot who has crash-landed in the desert encounters a mysterious boy who travels through the universe and eventually is persuaded to return to his own planet to tend a black rose he has planted there. Saint-Exupéry also wrote the very well regarded novel *Night Flight* (1931) and the prize-winning memoir *Wind, Sand, and Stars* (1939).

Below: Saint-Exupéry was determined to fly—perhaps destined for the skies.

Above: The Caudron Simoun plane just before take-off at Le Bourget—four hours later, the plane crashed in Libya's desert, but Saint-Exupéry and his flight engineer, Andre Prevot, survived (see box, page 57).

BORN TO FLY

Born in Lyon into an aristocratic family fallen on hard times, Saint-Exupéry attempted to go to the Ecole Navale, the French naval academy, but failed the entrance exams. He briefly studied architecture before joining the French air force in 1921. Five years later he became an airmail pilot for Aéropostale, flying over France, Spain, and northern Africa and, after 1929, in South America.

Saint-Exupéry spent the first part of World War II in the United States and Canada, and it was here that he wrote *The Little Prince*, in 1942. The following year he returned to Europe to fly reconnaissance missions for the Free French Air Force, based in North Africa. Aged 43, he was much older than most of the other pilots and was handicapped by poor mobility, due to pain from earlier crashes: he reputedly needed help to put on his flying suit and could not turn his head to the left to keep an eye out for attacking enemy aircraft. This inability to see properly what was going on around him may have been his undoing, but he flew eight successful missions before the fateful day on which he disappeared.

FINAL FLIGHT

On July 31, 1944, Saint-Exupéry took off in an unarmed Lockheed P-38 Lightning from Corsica, with instructions to perform reconnaissance of German troops in the Rhône Valley, France. He was never heard from again.

Various pieces of evidence point to what happened. The wreck of a P-38 was found by a diver in May 2000, on the seabed off the coast of Marseille, and was confirmed by experts in 2004 as Saint-Exupéry's aircraft. Today the remains of the aircraft are on display in the air and space museum at Le Bourget, Paris.

A body in French uniform, but which could not be identified, was washed up in September 1944, south of Marseille, and was buried in the cemetery at Carqueiranne. Then in September 1998 the pilot's silver identity bracelet was found near Riou Island, again, south of Marseille.

Below: Saint-Exupéry's wrecked P-38 plane is found and formally identified off the shore of Marseille, France.

PIECING IT TOGETHER

It is more or less certain, then, that Saint-Exupéry crashed off the coast of Marseille—but why? In 1948 former Luftwaffe airman Hermann Korth described an incident around midday on July 31, 1944, in which his aircraft engaged a P-38 in combat and shot it down. Since Saint-Exupéry's P-38 was an unarmed variant called the F-5, this is generally not thought to have been the incident that caused Saint-Exupéry to crash.

In 2008 another former Luftwaffe man, Horst Rippert, described how he thought he had shot down Saint-Exupéry, recalling that on July 31 he encountered a P-38 Lightning over the Mediterranean, near Marseille, and shot it down in flames. The remnants of the P-38 identified as belonging to Saint-Exupéry in 2004 did not contain bullet holes, but not all the wreckage was recovered.

Saint-Exupéry's squadron colleagues were devastated at the loss of their near-legendary comrade. For more than 70 years, and particularly in France, people have been troubled and captivated by the romantic story of the pilot hero who disappeared.

Below: The differing accounts of the two Luftwaffe men who thought they may have shot down Saint-Exupéry are inconclusive.

STRANGE
STORIES

Did the man who cheated death choose to die? In 1935 Saint-Exupéry and his navigator cheated death after crashing in the Libyan desert while attempting to set a new speed record. With only one day's worth of fluids, they survived for four days, becoming so dehydrated that they experienced vivid hallucinations. They were saved by a passing Bedouin who used a folk rehydration method. Later in the 1930s, Saint-Exupéry was asked which way he would prefer to die when the time came: he replied by drowning—saying that you don't feel you are dying, but rather like you are falling sleep and beginning to dream.

Probably because of his familiarity with death through so many close encounters, and because for so long there was no definitive evidence of where he was and why he disappeared, some claimed that Saint-Exupéry deliberately crashed on July 31, 1944. They pointed to the fact that in the English translation of

The Little Prince, the prince views the sunset on his planet 44 times a day: Saint-Exupéry disappeared aged 44 and in 1944. However, the narrative of a war hero, flying reconnaissance despite the pain of his battered body, and giving his life in the service of the Free French, remains the preferred version of accounts.

Above: Those who think the crash was deliberate point to eerie coincidences in *The Little Prince*.

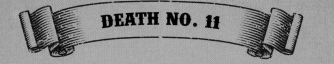

WHY DID GLENN MILLER FALL SILENT?

Date: December 15, 1944
Location: English Channel

Iconic American bandleader Glenn Miller went missing while flying across the English Channel to France in 1944. Neither his body nor the wreckage of the plane were ever found.

Glenn Miller was in Europe to entertain the troops. The hugely successful bandleader—famous for his recordings of "In the Mood," "Moonlight Serenade," "Chattanooga Choo Choo," and many others—had patriotically broken up his orchestra, enlisted in the army, and formed the Glenn Miller Army Air Force Band in the fall of 1942. In 1944 he brought the band to England, and on the fateful day of his disappearance was bound for Paris, which had recently been liberated from the Nazis, to play for the American servicemen there.

A HIT MUSICIAN

Born Alton Glenn Miller in 1904 in small-town Iowa, Miller began to make his way as a trombonist and arranger in the mid-to-late 1920s, playing for Ben Pollack's orchestra and then the Dorsey Brothers and Benny Goodman, among others. He established his first band in 1937 and a second in 1938. This orchestra, with its distinctive sound based on the clarinet and tenor sax delivering the melody and a group of saxophones providing harmony, was quickly a huge hit. By the next year, 1939, Miller had his own radio show three times a week. That same year he released the million-selling "Moonlight Serenade." By 1941 the band had hit Hollywood, appearing that year in the movie *Sun Valley Serenade*, which featured "Chattanooga Choo Choo," and then in 1942 in *Orchestra Wives*. Glenn Miller had 23 number 1 hits—more than Elvis (18) or the Beatles (20).

Above: Pictured here in *Billboard* magazine in 1942, Miller was at the height of his considerable fame.

Then in 1942, at the very height of his fame and when he was earning as much as $20,000 a week, Miller felt called to join the military and entertain American servicemen and women. He was turned down by the navy but accepted into the army and by 1944, when he brought the Army Air Force Band to London, he had the rank of colonel. The band gave 800 performances in England and made several recordings at Abbey Road Studios, London.

RALLYING THE TROOPS

Miller's broadcasts were used to raise morale among Allied troops—he was right up there with Bob Hope and the Andrews Sisters in this regard. They were also highly effective propaganda, some parts being broadcast in German across Europe. He famously said in one, "America means freedom, and there's no expression of freedom quite so sincere as music."

Just before Miller's disappearance, curiously, he and the band had cheated death when they narrowly escaped a German V1 flying bomb that hit the BBC Radio office, where they had been staying in Sloane Court, London, killing around 70 people. Miller and his band relocated to Bedford.

On December 15, 1944, Miller took off in a Noorduyn Norseman from an RAF base at Twinwood Farm, near Bedford. He was traveling with Lieutenant Colonel Norman Baessell—going ahead to make arrangements to transfer the band to France, with a view to playing concerts over Christmas. They were in the hands of pilot John Morgan. They never arrived at their destination in Paris.

THE SPECULATION

For some time, people thought that Miller's aircraft might have been hit by friendly fire—a casualty of unused bombs dropped by English aircraft over the Channel to lighten their load on the way home from a bombing raid. A fleet of 139 Lancaster bombers returning across the Channel at about 1:40 p.m. did drop bombs.

Above: The great American bandleader performs with his band. They gave more than 800 performances in England alone.

A navigator on one of the planes later said he saw a plane beneath while the bombs were being dropped, and saw the aircraft "go in"—that is, crash into the water. He said it was a Norseman, but some people were skeptical that an observer would have been able to recognize this aircraft in very poor visibility, since it was not a common type. These days, people generally reject this theory. US records suggest that the timing of the flights involved make it impossible.

The most likely explanation of what happened is that the plane crashed in poor visibility into the waters of the English Channel. It was close to midwinter and the conditions were brutal. One theory is that the carburetor in the aircraft's single engine iced up, causing the crash. The pilot would have had almost no chance of

saving the aircraft. Another is that they were flying low above the surface because of the very poor visibility and ice formed on the cockpit, causing the plane to smash into the waves.

Above: Could the Noorduyn Norseman have been hit by friendly fire coming from a fleet of Lancaster bombers?

One puzzling piece of information remains, however. This is the statement in a notebook kept by an amateur plane spotter named Richard Anderton. He states that he saw a Norseman, the plane that Miller took, flying to the west of London on December 15, 1944. This would mean the plane was heading in the wrong direction, away from Paris. Perhaps the pilot had got lost in the thick fog; perhaps there is something, after all, in the various conspiracy theories around the case (see box, opposite), and Miller was not heading to Paris at all.

Below: A Noorduyn Norseman plane just like the one that Miller took off in, bound for Paris.

─ STRANGE ─
STORIES

The total disappearance of Miller and the plane he was flying on, and the fact that the US military did not announce the bandleader's disappearance until December 24, nine days after the tragic event, have fueled conspiracy theories. One such theory is that he was captured and tortured by the Nazis. Another, that Miller was embroiled in an attempt to kill Nazi leader Adolf Hitler but was assassinated before he could pull it off. A colorful tale suggested that he had died mysteriously in the arms of a prostitute in a French brothel and the authorities covered it up to protect his reputation. Some even said he had fallen sick and returned in secret to the United States. Yet, for all the attraction of colorful theories, the likeliest story is the sad but simple one: that this great composer, performer, and bandleader was killed in a tragic accident in terrible weather conditions.

Above: Was Miller discovered to be involved in a plot to kill the Führer?

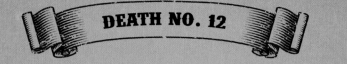

WAS RAOUL WALLENBERG SHOT BY THE KGB?

Date: Perhaps July 17, 1947
Location: Possibly in the Lubyanka building, Moscow, USSR

Swedish businessman and diplomat Raoul Wallenberg, the hero who saved thousands of Hungarian Jews from the Holocaust, disappeared while in Soviet captivity in 1947. Was he killed or did he live on for decades?

In the early years of World War II, Raoul Wallenberg was working for an import–export outfit, the Central European Trading Company, based in Stockholm, Sweden. His boss was a Hungarian Jew named Kalman Lauer; Wallenberg himself had a trace of Jewish inheritance from his Jewish great-great-grandfather and was proud of it. From 1938 the Jews in Hungary lived under a set of anti-Jewish laws—based on the Nuremberg Race Laws of Nazi Germany—that severely restricted their role in commercial and public life, and as it became very difficult for Lauer to travel to Hungary, Wallenberg took trips on his behalf.

Right: Wallenberg—the Swedish Schindler—led one of the most extensive and successful rescue efforts of the Nazi era.

Then in 1944 the Germans occupied Hungary and in April began rounding up Jews to deport them to extermination camps in Poland. Unlike many other aspects of the Nazis' Final Solution—their plan to exterminate the Jews—the persecution of the Hungarian Jews became known internationally. As part of a rescue effort, Wallenberg was sent by the Swedish government to the Hungarian capital, Budapest, on a diplomatic mission.

PROTECTIVE PASSPORTS

Wallenberg arrived in July. Around 435,000 Jews had already been sent to their deaths in the camps, but he managed to save as many as 35,000 more by giving "protective passports" to some and housing them in a group of rented buildings that he rehung with large Swedish flags and declared "extraterritorial" under the rules of diplomatic immunity. The passports, which said the people holding them were Swedish nationals awaiting repatriation, were not legal documents but were official-looking and, with the judicious use of bribes, were often accepted. Wallenberg did not work alone but as part of an international team that included Swiss and Portuguese diplomats and Giorgio Perlasca, an Italian posing as a Spanish diplomat and handing out fake Spanish documents.

Wallenberg was hands-on and pragmatic. He even rescued people from forced marches and trains headed for the death camps. In one celebrated incident, he intervened to haul people off a train set to depart for Auschwitz. He clambered onto the roof of the carriage and began handing his passports in through the door. He ignored the bullets of the Hungarian guards that were whistling over his head and, once he had handed out all the passports, clambered

Above: Wallenberg once intercepted an Auschwitz-bound train to save and help as many of its doomed occupants as possible.

down and ordered everyone who had been given one to get off the train and walk to a fleet of cars with Swedish colors that he had arranged to have parked nearby. When he had no more papers, he handed out food, clothing, and medicine.

The war turned against the Nazis, and before the end of the year the Soviet army besieged Budapest. It was in this period, before the city surrendered on February 13, 1945, that Wallenberg persuaded the Nazis not to carry through their plan to blow up the Budapest ghetto—and so saved the lives of the 70,000 Jews living there.

Then Wallenberg was seized by the Soviets on suspicion of espionage. It later became clear that Wallenberg, in addition to saving the Jews of Hungary, may have been working as an agent of the US Office of Strategic Services (the forerunner of the CIA); he had American contacts, having studied architecture at the University of Michigan before going to work at the Central European Trading Company. He was summoned to the Red Army headquarters of Marshal Rodion Malinovsky in Debrecen on January 17, 1945, but it's not clear what happened to him afterward.

Below: This "Schutz-Pass" (protection passport) saved the life of a young Jewish woman, Judith Kopstein, who was given it by Wallenberg on August 20, 1944.

One statement, on Soviet-controlled Hungarian radio on March 8, 1945, stated that Wallenberg and his driver were killed on the way to Debrecen, 120 miles (195 kilometers) east of the capital, yet there is pretty solid evidence that he made it to Debrecen, was then taken by train through Romania to Moscow, and imprisoned in the Lubyanka prison from January 21, 1945, onward. It seems that he shared a cell briefly with Gustav Richter, former aide to leading Nazi Adolf Eichmann, until Richter was moved on March 1 that year.

ALIVE IN THE EIGHTIES?

Various accounts seem to confirm that Wallenberg either died or
was executed by the KGB in 1947. A document released by the
Soviet government in 1957 stated that he had died suddenly in his
cell in Lubyanka on July 17, 1947, perhaps from a heart attack,
while in 1991 a Russian investigation found that Wallenberg had
been executed in Lubyanka in 1947. Around the same time, former
Soviet intelligence officer Pavel Sudoplatov stated that Wallenberg
was poisoned by assassin Grigory Mairanovsky. In 2016 the diary
of Ivan Serov, head of the KGB in 1954–58, was found: Serov
stated that Wallenberg had been executed in 1947. Wallenberg
was officially declared dead *in absentia* in Sweden in 2016.

Wallenberg was made an honorary citizen of Israel, Australia,
Hungary, Canada, and the United States, and in 2012 was
awarded a Congressional Gold Medal "in recognition of his
achievements and heroic actions during the Holocaust." Israel
also declared him one of the Righteous Among the Nations.

Below: The notorious
Lubyanka building, the
Russian secret service
official headquarters
in Moscow.

— STRANGE —
STORIES

Several people have claimed that Wallenberg may have remained alive in Soviet captivity long after his supposed death in 1947. Former German colonel and prisoner of war Theodor von Dufving claimed he met an imprisoned Swedish diplomat in Kirov in February 1949 who said he was there "through a great error," and British businessman Greville Wynne claimed to have spoken to a Swedish diplomat in Lubyanka in 1962, while another witness, Yefim Moshinsky, said he had encountered Wallenberg on Wrangel Island, a Soviet-held island in the Arctic Ocean, the same year. There were claims that he was still in Soviet prisons in the 1980s. His half-brother, physics professor Guy von Dardel, conducted official investigations into Wallenberg's fate and made around 50 research trips to the Soviet Union. He did not accept official versions of Wallenberg's death, but was never able to find conclusive evidence that he survived or died much later.

Above: Did Wallenberg make it to Wrangel Island in the Arctic Ocean?

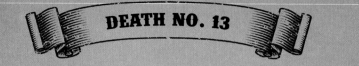
HOW DID HAROLD HOLT DIE ON A BEACH HE KNEW SO WELL?

Date: December 17, 1967
Location: Portsea, Victoria, Australia

Australian Prime Minister Harold Holt disappeared off Cheviot Beach, Victoria, in 1967. He was presumed to have died in the surf, but his body was never found, despite a dedicated search.

Harold Holt was a youthful 59 when he died. He was a keen swimmer, a devotee of water sports such as spearfishing, and said he knew Cheviot Beach, where he disappeared, "like the back of my hand." He was with friends, one of whom came partway into the water with him. So, how did he come to lose his life?

The likeliest explanation is that he simply misjudged how treacherous the hidden currents were on that day of rough seas in December 1967, that he overestimated his swimming ability, his capacity to resist the strength of the water. He was overwhelmed in a terrible accident.

The fact that his body was never found—despite the largest manhunt ever undertaken in Australia over the course of the following three weeks—and his prominent position as a world statesman led to the growth of a net of conspiracy theories.

Holt had become prime minister just under two years earlier, in January 1966. He was already a veteran politician, having entered parliament in 1935 as an MP for the United Australia Party. By 1940 he was a minister, then, in 1944, was a founder member of the newly established Liberal Party. He had served as deputy party leader and federal treasurer before becoming prime minister on the retirement of Robert Menzies.

Above: Holt enjoyed spearfishing and is pictured here at Portsea, near Melbourne, one year before his disappearance.

STORMY WATERS

On the day of his death, he had been at the cottage at Portsea, a resort near Melbourne, that he owned with his wife, Zara. He was there with Marjorie Gillespie, one of several women he was rumored to be having extramarital affairs with, along with her daughter, her daughter's boyfriend, and a family friend named Alan Stewart. They were returning from an outing to watch British sailor Alec Rose go past on his attempt to sail solo around the world, when they stopped at Cheviot Beach. It was the second beach they stopped at; the first had been closed by lifeguards because of the rough seas, but Cheviot Beach was unsupervised, so Holt could risk a swim.

One theory proposed in the period after his disappearance was that he might have been terminated by the CIA. Holt had made a public stand in support of US President Lyndon B. Johnson and American involvement in Vietnam, and in 1966, during a visit to the US, he promised that he would go "all the way with LBJ." He had pledged more than 6,000 Australian soldiers to support the US in Vietnam.

Left: Holt (left) had forged an alliance with Lyndon B. Johnson, which some think may have been the root cause of his death.

Above: Holt's clothes were left abandoned on Cheviot Beach.

Public opinion was hardening against this, and many Australians felt he had been too subservient to the US president in using the phrase that he did; the theory is that the CIA wanted to remove Holt before he backed down on the decision to support the Americans in Vietnam. However, the manner of his apparent death—only a short distance away from his watching friends—and the immense practical difficulty of CIA agents lying in wait for the prime minister in rough seas off Cheviot Beach make this seem extremely unlikely.

Another possibility is that Prime Minister Holt committed suicide, deliberately giving himself to the rip currents. Some claimed he had seemed low before the tragic day, but, again, the fact that he disappeared in front of a group of friends makes this proposal seem very unlikely. And those who knew him said he was renowned for taking pleasure in life and had a great deal to live for; he was not the type of person who would kill himself.

Left: A team of divers searched unsuccessfully for Holt's body, while a search party combed the beach.

Right: Perhaps one of the most outlandish theories is that the Australian premier was abducted by aliens, no doubt in a UFO.

A VISION OF DEATH

During the search for Holt's body, the authorities were contacted by an Indian guru who claimed to have had a vision of the prime minister's body on the seafloor. Divers were sent to the spot he described, but nothing was found. A high-profile memorial service was held on December 22, 1967, at St. Paul's Cathedral, Melbourne, while the search for Harold Holt was still ongoing. President Lyndon Johnson, Prince Charles, and British Prime Minister Harold Wilson all attended.

In September 2005, a coroner's inquiry dismissed the alternative theories about Harold Holt's death and ruled that the prime minister had drowned in rough seas. It is worth noting that he was being treated for a shoulder injury in the fall of 1967, and this may have affected his ability to resist the current and made him more vulnerable to being swept away. Today, a memorial plaque is sited on the seafloor near where he disappeared: "In memory of Harold Holt, Prime Minister of Australia, who loved the sea and disappeared hereabouts on December 17, 1967."

— STRANGE —
STORIES

Was he abducted by aliens? Vanished by China? Did he fake his own death so he could escape the responsibilities and duties of his position and start a new life with a lover? These were just three of the theories that were put forward following Harold Holt's disappearance. The China theory was proposed in a 1983 book, *The Prime Minister Was a Spy*, by British journalist Anthony Grey. He stated that Holt had been a spy for the Chinese government on and off since 1929, and that on the day he "died" at sea he was actually collected off Cheviot Beach by Chinese frogmen who helped him into a submarine that spirited him away to a new life. The book suggests Holt needed to escape because he believed Australian intelligence had become aware of his activities. Another theory was connected to the Vietnam War and suggested that Holt was assassinated by agents from North Vietnam.

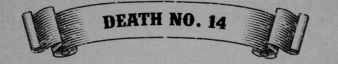

WHAT HAPPENED TO SEAN FLYNN?

Date: April 6, 1970
Location: Cambodia

American photojournalist Sean Flynn, son of Hollywood legend Errol Flynn, disappeared without a trace while working as a photojournalist in Cambodia for *Time* magazine in April 1970. Was he held prisoner? Was he executed?

Sean Flynn initially followed his swashbuckling father Errol Flynn into the movies. After appearing, aged 15, in his dad's TV show *The Errol Flynn Theatre*, he starred, aged 23, in the 1962 movie *The Son of Captain Blood*, a sequel to his father's 1935 hit *Captain Blood*, and, after that, in a few European productions, including *Stop Train 349*.

Sean had largely given up acting by 1966 and begun work as a freelance photojournalist. That year, he arrived in South Vietnam. His courage and willingness to put his body on the line in search of good shots meant that he was soon in demand, his work appearing in the magazines *Paris Match* and *Time* and being taken by UPI (United Press International). Colleagues of the time say he had something of the swashbuckling style of his father's movie characters. He was an eye-catching figure—tall, blue-eyed, wearing his blond hair long and with the sideburns that were then fashionable.

GROOVY DANGER

Sean Flynn undertook gung-ho missions and survived several close calls. He said at the time he "grooved on the danger," meaning the risk of combat and dangerous missions excited him. In April 1966 he was patrolling with Chinese soldiers and US Special Forces—the troops known as Green Berets—in South Vietnam when they were ambushed and he had to fight his way out, alongside the professionals, using an M-16 rifle.

In December that year he was with the 1st Brigade 101st Airborne Division, making a parachute jump. He was twice injured, in March 1966 and September 1968.

Above: Sean Flynn, combat photographer: pictured here ca. 1966, four years before his disappearance.

The day on which he vanished—April 6, 1970—he was traveling with fellow photographer Dana Stone, who was on assignment for CBS News, from the Cambodian capital Phnom Penh to Saigon (now known as Ho Chi Minh City) in Vietnam in order to attend an important press conference sponsored by the government. On the fateful day, the intrepid pair chose not to use the limousines favored by the main group of journalists, but instead to travel alone on motorcycles. And, on the lookout for a great picture, they rode into trouble. They had heard that there was a Viet Cong checkpoint on Highway 1 and, with typical audacity, deliberately took that route in the hope they could get some good images of Viet Cong guerrillas.

Above: The Viet Cong (Vietnamese Communists) were a guerrilla group that fought with the North Vietnamese army against the US and South Vietnam in the Vietnam War.

CHECKED OUT

We know that they were taken hostage by the guerrillas at the checkpoint but, after that, all is a blank—despite long and intensive searches funded by Sean's mother, the French-American actress Lili Damita.

The latest thinking is that Flynn and Stone were seized in Svay Rieng province and held in captivity for more than a year. The two journalists were probably marched northward. It seems the captives began to slow the troops down and were handed over to the Cambodian communists, the Khmer Rouge, who executed them in June 1971. Experts suggest that the Viet Cong did not normally kill journalists, preferring to release them with the aim of passing positive propaganda around, but it would have been a different story with the Khmer Rouge.

For years, Lili Damita refused to give up in her search for her lost son, who was only 28 years old when he disappeared. However, eventually she admitted defeat and had him declared legally dead in 1984. Former colleagues and interested journalists kept up the search, and a 2010 TV movie suggested his body might have turned up (also see box, opposite), but Sean's death remains unsolved.

— STRANGE —
STORIES

In 2010 researchers thought they had found Flynn's body when they dug up what were apparently the remains of a Western hostage who had been killed by the Khmer Rouge at a site at Phka Dong village, Kampong Cham province, eastern Cambodia. They were led to the site by a local man who said he had witnessed the killing of a blond-haired foreigner there many years earlier. The local said the victim had been made to dig his own grave and then gruesomely battered to death with a rock after the gun intended for his execution jammed. Laboratory tests on the remains carried out by the Joint POW/MIA Accounting Command (JPAC), the US Department of Defense body tasked with identifying the remains of Americans listed as Missing in Action or PoWs, said there was no match with samples of Flynn's DNA they had on file. Whose remains were they? JPAC said they were of an indigenous person. Nevertheless, British photographer Tim Page, former colleague of Flynn and Stone, has said that he thought the site in question might contain the remains of Western journalists and that local people had said graves there held the bodies of several foreigners.

Above: Flynn's DNA did not match that of the remains dug up in eastern Cambodia in 2010. The search for his body continues.

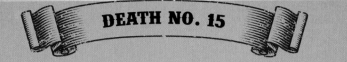

WHO KILLED DR. GONZO?

Date: May 1974
Location: Mazatlán, Mexico

Larger-than-life Chicano activist Oscar Zeta Acosta—the inspiration for Hunter S. Thompson's character "Dr. Gonzo"—disappeared without a trace in Mexico in 1974.

Oscar Zeta Acosta was a lawyer, novelist, and activist in the Chicano Movement, or *El Movimiento*, promoting civil rights for Mexican Americans. The self-styled "Brown Buffalo" was a powerfully built, colorful figure who wore decorated ties and whose floral briefcase bore a "Chicano Power" sticker. He once attended court barefoot and, on another occasion, in company with his friend Hunter S. Thompson, pioneer of "Gonzo journalism," set fire to a judge's lawn during a trial. As "Dr. Gonzo," he was a key character in Thompson's celebrated 1972 novel *Fear and Loathing in Las Vegas*.

Born in Texas but raised in Riverbank, California, Acosta joined the US Air Force, then studied creative writing at San Francisco State University before becoming a lawyer in Oakland in 1966. He met Thompson in 1967 and in the following year moved to southern California to join the Chicano Movement, working as an activist lawyer. He was among the attorneys who defended the "Eastside 13," a group secretly indicted for organizing educational walkouts and marches in 1968 to protest poor conditions in mainly Latino schools in Los Angeles. Each defendant faced 66 years in prison, but Acosta and the other defense lawyers succeeded in arguing that the protest organizers were exercising their First Amendment rights. In 1971 Thompson wrote about Acosta's work in east LA for *Rolling Stone* magazine.

While holding discussions for this piece, the pair determined to make a trip to Las Vegas in order to escape police and local community attention and so be freer to talk openly about racial tensions in LA and the death of Mexican-American *LA Times* journalist Ruben Salazar, killed on an anti-Vietnam War march

Below: The legend lives on: a local artist paints a mural of Acosta on the wall of a performing arts center, 2018.

Above: The death of journalist Ruben Salazar during an anti-Vietnam War march became a common focus for Acosta and Thompson.

in 1970 after being struck by a projectile containing teargas fired by an LA County Sheriff's deputy. Salazar's death was one of the principal subjects of Thompson's 19,200-word *Rolling Stone* piece, "Strange Rumblings in Aztlan." Thompson and Acosta's trip to Nevada was the focus of *Fear and Loathing in Las Vegas*, in which the lawyer was transformed into "Dr. Gonzo, a 300-pound Samoan."

"ONE OF GOD'S OWN PROTOTYPES"

Acosta was charismatic, unconventional, audacious, and multitalented. Before his disappearance in 1974 he had left the Roman Catholic Church into which he had been born and become a Baptist pastor; he ran for LA County sheriff in 1970, but lost to Peter J. Pitchess; and he published two novels, *Autobiography of a Brown Buffalo* (1972) and *The Revolt of the Cockroach People* (1973).

He was an enthusiastic drug user: Thompson said he had an addiction to amphetamines and liked to take LSD, and that the combination of "a 250-pound Mexican and LSD-25" was a "potentially terminal menace." In the introduction he wrote to Acosta's novel *The Revolt of the Cockroach People*, Thompson said that the author was "a wild boy" who brought a "terrible joy" with him, adding that he was "one of God's own prototypes."

In May 1974 Acosta went missing while traveling in Mexico. He telephoned his son, Marco Acosta, from Mazatlán and told him he was about to board a boat. He headed out into the ocean and was never heard from again. Many theories swirled around his disappearance. Some people argued that he was shot when a drug bust went wrong. Others suggested he had a nervous breakdown, possibly drug-induced. Marco later said that in all likelihood, "knowing the people he was involved with," he got in an argument and was killed in a brawl.

STRANGE STORIES

We don't know what happened to the "Brown Buffalo" and, as with other cases of unsolved disappearances in this book, such as Butch Cassidy and the Sundance Kid (see page 26) or Harold Holt (see page 70), some people refused to believe he had died, and decided he had gone underground. His friend Thompson would receive letters from people claiming to have spotted him long after his apparent date of death in 1974. Sightings were reported all over the globe—one popular theory was that he had returned to the US and was living in Miami. Thompson addressed some of these rumors in another *Rolling Stone* piece "The Banshee Screams for Buffalo Meat," published December 15, 1977, in which he wrote of the missing activist that he was "too weird to live and too rare to die." He certainly had an afterlife in the movies, being played by Peter Boyle in the 1980 picture *Where the Buffalo Roam*, with Bill Murray as Thompson and directed by Art Linson, and by Benicio del Toro in the 1997 movie adaptation of *Fear and Loathing in Las Vegas*, with Johnny Depp as Thompson and directed by Terry Gilliam. Del Toro later produced a 2017 documentary picture, *The Rise and Fall of the Brown Buffalo*, directed by Phillip Rodriguez.

Above: Whether or not Acosta lived on in real life, cult movies such as *Fear and Loathing in Las Vegas* have immortalized the "300-pound Samoan."

KILLERS UNKNOWN

In books, TV, and cinema, we love a good "whodunit." Detective dramas usually leave little doubt as to where the body is; what is often uncertain is who carried out the killing, how, and why. Budding detectives concentrate on means (how the killer terminated the victim), motive (did the accused killer have a reason to kill?), and opportunity (did the accused killer have the chance to do the dastardly deed?). In fiction the case is usually solved, but in the real, historical world there are many cases of unsolved murder—from papal princes and royals to modern-day journalists—in which we puzzle over the holy trinity of means, motive, and opportunity, but are unable to determine with any finality who did the deed.

Left: The intrigue of Mary Rogers' death inspired a short story by the father of the detective narrative, Edgar Allan Poe.

When Giovanni Borgia—son of a dissolute pope, scion of one of history's most infamous families, and a man with many enemies—was stabbed and his body thrown into the Tiber River in 1497, there were many possible perpetrators. By contrast, the evidence in the killing of Lord Darnley, husband of Mary Queen of Scots, in 1567, all seemed to point to one man: the queen's reputed lover, the 4th Earl of Bothwell. This was never proved, but it sparked a scandal that brought both Bothwell and Mary to ruin. In some puzzling cases, there does not seem to be a clear motive for anyone. The drowning of New York's "beautiful cigar girl," Mary Rogers, in 1841, is a case in point, and, like so many unfortunate others, her death has given rise to dramatic stories and endless speculation.

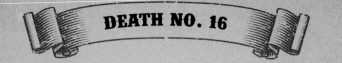

WHO KILLED GIOVANNI BORGIA?

Date: June 14, 1497
Location: Rome, Italy

In the heart of Rome, the Pope's son was found dumped unceremoniously in the Tiber River, with his throat cut. Was he murdered by his own brother?

It was the Renaissance equivalent of a high-society murder. The body of Giovanni Borgia—son of Pope Alexander VI, one of the world's most powerful men—was dragged from the Tiber River in Rome, with nine stab wounds and a cut throat.

Giovanni was last seen leaving a party thrown in his honor by his mother at her villa, attended by his sister, Lucrezia, and brothers, Cesare and Gioffre. His horse had returned home without its rider, one of its stirrups having been cut. A search party was sent out. It was June 14, 1497.

Right: Giovanni Borgia, like many members of his clan, was rumored to be a decadent womanizer, a reputation that would fuel the posthumous speculation on the cause of his brutal death.

When Giovanni's butchered body was found, his purse was intact and contained the very substantial sum of 30 gold ducats. It could not have been a robbery—otherwise cutting the purse strings would have been the assailant's first move. Was it a crime of passion? A cold-blooded assassination? Giovanni's only attendant was also killed, so there was no eyewitness testimony as to what had really happened.

WORLD AT HIS FEET

The victim had been raised to a high position by his father's predilection for nepotism—scheming to advance family members to positions of power. Through his father's machinations, Giovanni had married Maria Enríquez, cousin of King Ferdinand II of Aragon, and been made Duke of Gandía in Spain. He was also Gonfalonier and Captain General of the Church, meaning he was commander of the papal forces at a time when the Roman Catholic Church was a major political player and not averse to engaging in military conflict.

Below: Initially, Pope Alexander VI did seem rocked by the murder of his son Giovanni and made some effort to amend his ways, but not for long.

Giovanni's father, Pope Alexander VI, was an ambitious and worldly man who was seemingly entirely unashamed by the discrepancy between his dissolute, self-interested lifestyle and his

position as leader of the Church and, in this period before the Protestant Reformation, of all Christians in the Western world. Priests and churchmen were supposed to live celibate lives, but Alexander VI openly acknowledged his four children by his principal mistress Vannozza dei Cattanei. He had 11 children in all. As Rodrigo de Borgia, he had had a long career in the church, and built up a vast personal fortune, before being elected Pope on August 11, 1492, aged 61. He lived in the style of a Renaissance prince and, while still a cardinal, earned a reprimand from Pope Pius II in 1460 for scandalous behavior associated with a garden party in Siena. He effectively bought the position of

Pope—bribing Cardinal Ascanio Sforza, whose vote brought about the necessary two-thirds majority, with four mule-loads of silver. Nevertheless—and despite the fact that he was not Italian but Spanish, born near Valencia in 1431—his election to the papacy was popular with the people of Rome.

The death of Giovanni temporarily stunned the Pope into piety. He declared, "We loved the duke of Gandía more than any other person in the world ... God has done this as a punishment for our wrongdoings. We on our account are determined to mend our own life and to begin reform of the Church." He had a bill drafted to ban concubinage (the practice of priests living as if married with women) and simony (selling and buying church positions and favors)—both sins of which he was very much guilty. He also called an investigation into his son's bloody death, but he soon reverted to his wicked ways. And the investigation was abruptly canceled after a week.

Above: The Roman people lit bonfires and even held a bullfight in the square in front of St. Peter's to celebrate the appointment of Pope Alexander VI.

Above: Did Cesare (left) kill his own brother, jealous that Giovanni, too, was a lover of their sister Lucrezia (pictured here standing between Cesare and her father)?

MULTIPLE SUSPECTS

The killer was never identified, and historians have various theories as to who was responsible. The most popular theory is that Giovanni was killed by or on the orders of his brother Cesare. Cesare was utterly ruthless, powerfully ambitious, and far keener on hunting and womanizing than the church affairs he should have been attending to when made a cardinal and Archbishop of Valencia while still in his teens. They said he was the most handsome man in Italy, and he must have traded on this, as he had syphilis in his early twenties.

Cesare certainly profited from Giovanni's death, for he took his brother's position as commander of the papal armies. Some say both he and Giovanni were lovers of their sister Lucrezia, and that Cesare was driven by jealousy. Other suggestions are that Giovanni Sforza, Lucrezia's husband, or another Borgia brother, Gioffre, were behind the killing—with jealousy again the motive. Another theory is that members of the Orsini clan were the killers. They may have learned that the Pope was about to grant some of their territories to Giovanni; they were opponents of the Borgias, and three Orsini brothers would later be co-conspirators in a failed 1502 plot against Cesare Borgia.

Such was the unholy decadence of the Borgia clan that people have found it all too easy to believe that two brothers were in love with their sister and that one killed the other out of jealousy arising from this incestuous love triangle. Some years later—after the death of Pope Alexander VI in 1503—Giovanni's wife added weight to this theory by accusing Cesare of killing her husband.

— STRANGE —
STORIES

Cesare, Giovanni Borgia's brother, was also stabbed to death by unidentified assailants. In charge of the papal forces after the death of Giovanni, he embarked on a campaign to subjugate the cities of central Italy. The death of his father, from malaria, in 1503, brought his campaign to a shuddering halt: the next Pope, Julius II, was a major opponent of the Borgias and had Cesare arrested and jailed in Spain. He escaped and took arms to fight in the service of his brother-in-law, King John of Navarre. They besieged a rebel nobleman, Luis de Beaumont, in his castle at Viana, Navarre, but after Luis managed to smuggle supplies in during a great storm, Cesare set out after the supplying party, now in retreat. He rode on too eagerly, far ahead of his companions, and was then ambushed by the men he had set out to attack. Not realizing who he was, they pulled him from his horse, stripped him naked, and stabbed him no fewer than 25 times. He was found in a rocky stretch of countryside having bled to death and

Above: Cesare also met a gruesome end, just like his brother, while beseiging the castle at Viana, Navarre, northern Spain.

was buried in a humble local church beneath the stirring epitaph: "Here beneath a scant stretch of earth lies the man all the world feared."

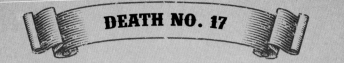

WHO MURDERED LORD DARNLEY?

Date: February 8–9, 1567
Location: Edinburgh, Scotland

The husband of Mary, Queen of Scots, was found dead, apparently strangled, in Edinburgh. Who was behind the deadly attack?

The bodies of Lord Darnley and his valet William Taylor were found in the orchard of Kirk o'Field, a two-story house near Holyrood Abbey, Edinburgh, on February 9, 1567. Shortly before, two explosions had rocked the house, but the bodies showed no sign of having been injured in the explosion—they were thought to have been strangled. The principal victim was just 21.

Lord Darnley was the cousin and second husband of Mary, Queen of Scots. They had married two years earlier in 1565. Mary Stuart had become Queen of Scotland at just six days old, when her father, King James V, died. She had later married Francis, heir to the French throne, and, after he became King Francis II, reigned as queen consort in France. Francis II died in 1560, and Mary returned to Scotland in 1561.

Above: Lord Darnley (left) was more than 6 feet tall, unusual for the time, and said to be strikingly handsome, at least according to Mary (right).

TALL, HANDSOME HUSBAND

Mary was much taken with Darnley—when he presented himself to her in 1565, she said (according to Scottish diplomat James Melville), that he was "the lustiest and best proportioned long man she had seen." They married in a Roman Catholic ceremony at Holyrood on July 29, 1565.

Both the English-born Darnley and Mary were grandchildren of Margaret Tudor, sister of Henry VIII, and so had a decent claim to the English throne; they represented a threat to the reigning English Queen, Henry's daughter, Elizabeth I. Darnley and Mary were soon estranged, not least because Darnley was involved in the brutal murder of Mary's secretary, David Riccio, on March 9, 1566. Darnley's drunkenness and uncouth behavior at court also made him many enemies. Nevertheless, the couple had a son, born June 19 that year, who would become King James VI of Scotland and eventually James I of England. In the months after the birth, Darnley and Mary appeared to be moving toward a reconciliation.

BEGINNING OF THE END

The death of Darnley caused a royal scandal. Shortly before the killing, Mary had brought Darnley to Kirk o'Field from Glasgow, where he had been recuperating from smallpox (or possibly syphilis). On the night of the murder, Mary was absent, attending the wedding of one of her servants in Holyrood.

Suspicion fell on James Hepburn, 4th Earl of Bothwell, who was known to be ambitious and had been in close attendance on the queen—some said they were sexually intimate. The shoes of one of his supporters were found at the scene of the murder and a soldier in Bothwell's pay, William Blackadder, was first at the scene. With indecent haste, Bothwell and Mary left Edinburgh. One account had it that he carried her off to Dunbar Castle, where he raped her; but another version had it that she went willingly. Only three months after Darnley's death, Mary married Bothwell.

William Blackadder swore his innocence, but was denounced by people who needed to remain anonymous, and convicted. He was hung, drawn, and quartered. The Casket Letters—eight letters and poems written by Mary to Bothwell and found in a silver casket— were produced by the couple's opponents, to indicate that Mary supported Darnley's killing, although historians generally agree they were forgeries.

An uprising led to Mary's abdication in favor of her son James, and she fled to England to seek the protection of Elizabeth I. Bothwell escaped to Scandinavia, was imprisoned at Dragsholm Castle in Denmark, and died in April 1578. Mary was kept under lock and key in northern England, a potential threat to Elizabeth I's rule as a figurehead for those plotting to replace Protestant Elizabeth with a Roman Catholic monarch. Finally, she was implicated in the Babington Plot to assassinate Elizabeth, convicted, and executed on February 8, 1587.

Below: The extent of Mary's involvement in Darnley's death is uncertain, but she may have had a motive.

— STRANGE —
STORIES

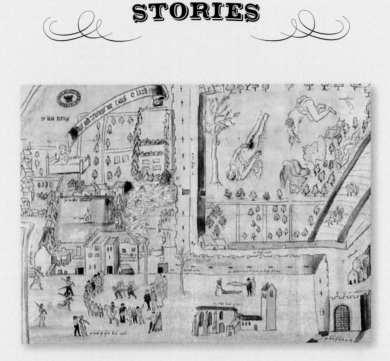

Some say the earls of Morton and Moray were the masterminds of Darnley's murder, and were merely using Bothwell to promote Moray's interests in the royal circle. The Earl of Moray was an illegitimate son of James V—and after Mary's abdication became Regent of Scotland on behalf of her son, the infant James VI. In this way he clearly benefited from the death of Darnley and Mary's disgrace, but he was assassinated in 1570 by one of Mary's supporters. Afterward, his partner in

Above: This drawing of Kirk o'Field was made after the murder of Lord Darnley, and shows where the victim's body lay.

crime, the Earl of Morton, became regent in his place. Another noble suspect embroiled in the plot was the leading lawyer Lord Pittendreich, an unscrupulous former favorite and secretary of Mary's, who arranged for Darnley to be lodged at Kirk o'Field and purchased the gunpowder used in the explosion.

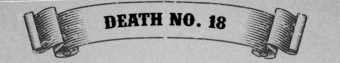
WHO KILLED MARY ROGERS?

Date: July 1841
Location: New York

When the body of a celebrated New York beauty was found in the Hudson River it caused a national sensation—and inspired an Edgar Allan Poe short story.

Below: Mary became known as the "Beautiful Cigar Girl."

The Mary Rogers case was front-page news. The victim was a widely celebrated beauty who attracted well-known authors to the cigar shop where she worked, including Washington Irving, who pioneered use of the name "Gotham" for New York City, and James Fenimore Cooper, who wrote *The Last of the Mohicans*. A poem about her comely appearance had been printed in the *New York Herald*. Mary lived with her widowed mother, Phoebe, who took to running a boarding house after her husband, Mary's father, was killed in a steamboat explosion.

Mary's disappearance in 1841 was the second time she had gone missing—three years earlier the press had been full of the news of her having gone out and left a suicide note, but she returned safe and sound, having apparently been no farther than Brooklyn, and the sequence of events was dismissed by some as a stunt to sell newspapers and promote her boss's cigar shop. By 1841 she was engaged to be married. Her fiancé was Daniel Payne, a cork-cutter who boarded in her mother's house. On July 25, 1841, she told him she was leaving on a trip to visit her aunt in New Jersey.

Above: Mary's boss, John Anderson, paid her a good wage to work in his Liberty Street cigar shop because her beauty attracted so much custom.

Left: This illustration—from the short story *The Mystery of Marie Rogêt*, by Edgar Allan Poe—shows Mary's corpse being dragged from the river.

She told her mother she would be back on the next day. That night, a heavy storm struck New York City. Mary did not return as promised on July 26. Initially, her mother thought she had been delayed by disruption caused by the storm, but she quickly became worried and placed a notice in the *Sun* newspaper, appealing to anyone who had seen Mary to ask her to contact her mother at the boarding house.

FLOATING BODY FOUND

The following day, three days after she had left, her corpse was found floating in the Hudson River, near Sybil's Cave in Hoboken, New Jersey. Walking on the shore, a group of friends noticed an object bobbing in the water and, hiring a boat, rowed out to investigate. They found it was a young woman's body and pulled her in to the shore. A former fiancé—not Daniel Payne—

identified the corpse as Mary. Later the coroner's report recorded that Mary's body looked as if it had been beaten. What's more, the young woman's coat and hat had been torn. So, the initial evidence suggested Mary had been attacked, but the coroner noted—importantly, in view of what was later suggested—that this was the body of "a person of chastity and correct habits." The young woman had not been pregnant.

The case was covered in detail on the front pages of the *Sun*, *Tribune*, and *Herald* newspapers. American writer Edgar Allan Poe even reworked the details of the case into a detective story, *The Mystery of Marie Rogêt*, set in Paris. The story was the sequel to his earlier work, *The Murders in the Rue Morgue*, which was the first published detective story—and, like the earlier work, it featured C. Auguste Dupin, forerunner of later fictional detectives from Sherlock Holmes onward. Poe's Marie Rogêt was the first detective story based on true events: he was quite open about his story being based on the Mary Rogers case and declared in a letter, "under the pretense of showing how Dupin ... unraveled the mystery of Marie's assassination, I, in fact, enter into a very rigorous analysis of the real tragedy in New York." In Poe's story Marie is a worker in a perfume shop whose body is found in the River Seine in Paris; Dupin concludes she was murdered by a single murderer and dumped into the water from a moving boat.

Below: Poe's *Marie Rogêt* was the first detective story based on true events.

REAL-LIFE THEORIES

Back in the real world, one initial theory was that her fiancé, Daniel Payne, had done away with her—perhaps she had declared she wanted to leave him and he had preferred to kill her than allow another man to love her—but he had a solid alibi for the night on which she was killed. Another idea was that she had been attacked by a criminal gang who killed her, robbed her, and threw her body in the river. In late August some items of women's clothing were found by boys in the woods in Hoboken. The condition of the clothes suggested that they had been lying around there for three or four weeks—about the right amount of time to be Mary's. What's more, one of them was a handkerchief embroidered "M. R."

NATIONAL POLICE GAZETTE.

Vol. 2. No. 27—92 A YEAR.   NEW-YORK, SATURDAY, MARCH 13, 1847.   FOUR CENTS A NUMBER.

THE FEMALE ABORTIONIST.

Above: Abortionist Ann Lohman, better known as "Madame Restell," was a self-professed doctor and pharmacist who was linked to Mary's death in a deathbed confession.

The mother of the boys who found the clothes, Frederica Loss, was the owner of a local inn. Interviewed in the press, she now said she had seen Mary in the vicinity on July 25 with a stranger and the couple had even ordered lemonade at the inn. Then, later on, she had heard a scream from the woods. At first, she feared it was one of her sons and ran out to look, but she saw nothing and so, assuming the noise to have been made by an animal, did no more. However, Loss's later deathbed confession linked an abortionist to Mary's death (see box, opposite).

No further evidence was found. The general consensus was that Mary had been attacked and killed by criminals.

— STRANGE —
STORIES

The Mary Rogers case had two further twists in the tail. In October 1841 Daniel Payne killed himself. At the end of a drinking spree he made his way to Hoboken and the place where Mary's body had been dragged ashore from the Hudson. There he took laudanum and died, leaving a note: "To the world— Here I am on the very spot. God forgive me for my misspent life." Was he making a confession? Had he been involved in Mary's death? Or was he merely heartbroken to have lost her?

Then one year later, in October 1842, Federica Loss made a deathbed confession. She said she had known "the stranger" with whom she had seen Mary: the couple were at the inn for Mary to have a "premature delivery"— that is, for the man to perform a backstreet abortion—which went wrong and Mary died. Loss's sons helped clean up, slipping the body into the river and scattering items of Mary's clothes in the woods. This does not explain why Mary's body, when it was discovered, seemed to have been beaten, but it convinced many, not least because backstreet abortions were a matter of concern at the time.

Left: Daniel Payne's body was found at Sybil's Cave, near to where his fiancé's body had been found just months before.

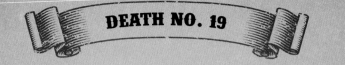

WAS THE "FATHER OF CINEMATOGRAPHY" MURDERED?

Date: September 16, 1890
Location: Between Dijon and Paris, France

Frenchman Louis Le Prince disappeared in 1890, and his body was never found. Did Thomas Edison, his rival in the development of cinematography, order his killing?

French motion-picture pioneer Louis Le Prince may have been the victim of cut-throat competition in the early days of cinema. He disappeared without a trace from a train between Dijon and Paris, on September 16, 1890. As a result, he was not able to demonstrate his motion-picture equipment in the US, and one theory about his death is that he was eliminated by a hitman working for Thomas Edison.

Born in Metz, France, Le Prince became interested in photography early in life. After studying art and chemistry, he moved to Yorkshire, northern England, and married. With his wife, he established the Leeds Technical School of Art.

WORLD'S OLDEST FILM

After a spell living in the US, where he began to develop a 16-lens motion-picture camera, Le Prince returned to Yorkshire in 1887 and, the following year, filmed a short sequence of moving pictures at Oakwood Grange in Roundhay, Leeds, which is celebrated as the world's oldest surviving film. For *Roundhay Garden Scene*, Le Prince used a single-lens camera of his own design. He was well ahead of other celebrated pioneers.

After *Roundhay Garden Scene* Le Prince made a film of traffic crossing Leeds Bridge, the first motion-picture sequence to be projected onto a screen. Le Prince had been granted a US patent on a 16-lens camera and projector, and applied for similar in the UK, where he also applied for a patent on his single-lens device.

Below: *Roundhay Garden Scene* lasts for just over two seconds and shows four people—including Le Prince's 16-year-old son, Adolphe—walking around in a garden.

The year Le Prince planned a public demonstration of his equipment in New York City, 1890, he disappeared. He was on the first stage of his journey.

DISAPPEARING ACT

Neither Le Prince's body nor his luggage were ever found. Seven years later, in 1897, he was declared dead. In 2003 a photograph of a drowned man from 1890 was found in police archives in Paris and it is said to look like Le Prince.

Various theories have been put forward as to what happened to the cinematographer. One is that he killed himself because he was about to go bankrupt. Le Prince's great-nephew told film historian Georges Potonniée that this is what happened. However, there is no evidence that he was in financial difficulty—his business was thriving and he had a great deal to look forward to.

Another idea is that Le Prince's family persuaded him to disappear and start a new life. Journalist Léo Sauvage says he was shown a note by the director of the Dijon Library indicating that, at his family's urging, Le Prince took off for the US because he was secretly homosexual, and that he died in 1898 in Chicago—but there is no evidence that Le Prince was gay.

A third proposal was that his brother killed him. The two had met in Dijon, where his brother lived, in order to sort out their mother's will—and for Louis to pick up his share of his inheritance before heading off to the US. Did they quarrel, and did it end in Louis' bloody death?

Above: Le Prince was ahead of his game—and his peers, leading some to ask whether he was murdered by his rivals in the nascent motion-picture business.

Right: Whether he had any involvement or not in Le Prince's disappearance, Edison stood to gain from losing his foremost competitor in the invention of cinematography.

─ STRANGE ─
STORIES

In 2008 graduate Alexis Bedford found a notebook among some of Thomas Edison's papers in the archives of New York Library, which appeared to contain notes acutely relevant to Le Prince's disappearance and written in Edison's handwriting. Under the date September 20, 1890, the journal entry states:

"Eric called me today from Dijon. It has been done. Prince is no more." So, did Edison arrange the killing of his rival? We will never know for sure. Historian Robert Myre later authenticated the book as genuine and the handwriting as Edison's.

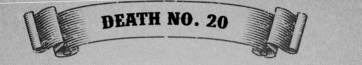

DEATH NO. 20

DID INSURANCE SALESMAN WILLIAM WALLACE KILL HIS WIFE?

Date: January 20, 1931
Location: Liverpool, England

Liverpool insurance salesman William Wallace said he was on a business call when his wife was killed. He was convicted of her murder, and jailed, but later freed on appeal.

William Wallace's wife, Julia, was beaten to death in the sitting room of their house at 29 Wolverton Street in the Anfield district of Liverpool, northern England, on the evening of Tuesday, January 20, 1931. Her unsolved death is one of the most famous cases in British judicial history. Several crime novelists, including Dorothy L. Sayers, Raymond Chandler, and P. D. James have written about it. It has been called "the perfect murder," a "classic of criminology," "a stalemate," and "the case where everything is canceled out by something else." Chandler wrote: "I call it the impossible murder because Wallace couldn't have done it and neither could anyone else."

The previous evening, Wallace was at the Liverpool Central Chess Club, where he was given a telephone message that had been left around 25 minutes before he arrived by one "R. M. Qualtrough," asking him to make a business call to 25 Menlove Gardens East, South Liverpool, at 7:30 p.m. on Tuesday 20. He later said he traveled across the city by tram to keep the appointment, only to find that the address did not exist—he asked several people, including a local policeman, but found that although there were Menlove Gardens West, South, and North, there was no such place as Menlove Gardens East. He even tried calling at 25 Menlove Gardens West, but the residents there had not heard of Mr. Qualtrough. After looking for around 45 minutes, so at about 8:15 p.m., Wallace returned home.

Below: Could the unassuming insurance salesman have committed the perfect murder? It seems unlikely, but then, if he didn't, who did?

His next-door neighbors, the Johnstons, happened to meet him at 8:45 p.m. on the street outside his home. He said he was unable to get in at front or back, but while they watched he tried again and found he could get in through the back door. There he found Julia lying on the floor of the front room, on top of a mackintosh and in front of the gas fire, her head having been bashed in.

UNDER SUSPICION

The police investigation initially found the time of Julia's death to be 8 p.m. They discovered that the telephone box from which the "R.M. Qualtrough" call had been made was not near Menlove Gardens North, South, or West, but rather just 400 yards (365 meters) away from Wallace's home. They became convinced that Wallace had made the call himself, although the person who received the call at the Chess Club insisted that the caller had not been Wallace.

The violent assault on Julia Wallace would have produced a great deal of blood, but there was no evidence of this on Wallace's suit, which he had been wearing on the night of the murder. The police came up with the theory that he had stripped naked and worn only the mackintosh that was found beneath his wife's body when making the attack. However, they also found, when they inspected the drains and bath, that there was no evidence of blood having been washed off—except for a single clot of blood in the toilet pan—which was never properly explained.

Right: The telephone call from "R.M. Qualtrough," asking Wallace to call in at 25 Menlove Gardens East on the evening of the fatal attack, proved pivotal to the case.

The police also suggested that it would have been possible for Wallace to commit the murder and then catch the tram he took to Menlove Gardens. They proved this by using a young, fit detective who sprinted from the house to the tram stop, whereas Wallace was 52 years old and not in good health. Puzzlingly, the police then adjusted the time of death from 8 p.m. to 6:30 p.m.

Wallace was arrested two weeks later. He maintained his innocence, but was convicted in court. Then in May 1931 the Court of Criminal Appeal overturned the verdict on the basis that it was "not supported by the weight of evidence," and set him free. Wallace went back to his job in insurance but found that people were so suspicious of him that he could not make a living. He transferred to a clerical job that did not require face-to-face interactions. He also moved from Anfield to the village of Bromborough on the Wirral Peninsula, across the River Mersey from Liverpool.

Above: To escape the suspicions and be able to continue making a living, Wallace moved from Wolverton Street in Anfield across the Mersey River to Bromborough in the Wirral.

Left: The victim of the "perfect murder"; Julia Wallace's death remains as unsolved as it is intriguing.

Right: Perhaps the key to the case lies—now in the grave—with a former dishonest colleague who had worked alongside Wallace at the Prudential.

Wallace did not enjoy his freedom for long. He died in a hospital just two years later, in February 1933, from complications associated with kidney trouble. Difficulty with his kidneys had forced him to return to England from Shanghai in 1907, where he had been working for a military outfitter, and to have his left kidney removed at Guy's Hospital, London.

No one else was ever charged with Julia Wallace's murder, which remains officially an unsolved case. The murder weapon was never found.

— STRANGE —
STORIES

Did Wallace's former colleague commit the murder? In the 1960s Jonathan Goodman's book on the case focused on a man who had worked with Wallace at the Prudential insurance company before the murder. Wallace had found that this man, whom Goodman did not name, had not been paying in the premiums he collected from his customers. Although Wallace did not report him to the company, the man left under a cloud. The man was named, by radio journalist Roger Wilkes in a 1981 program about the case, as Richard Gordon Parry. Wilkes discovered that a young woman had given Parry an alibi for the time of the murder but later withdrew it. In addition, Parry had visited a garage on the evening of the murder and washed his car with a pressure hose. One of the garage employees had noticed that one of Parry's gloves was stained with blood. His supposed motive was to steal the day's premiums left at home by Wallace while he tried to find Menlove Gardens East. Parry died in 1980.

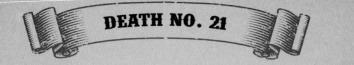

WAS ACTRESS CHRISTA HELM KILLED FOR WHAT SHE KNEW?

Date: February 12, 1977
Location: West Hollywood, Los Angeles, California

The actress and model, who allegedly kept a sex diary of her famous conquests, was found bludgeoned to death in Hollywood. Who was behind her killing?

Aspiring actor and model Christa Helm was found stabbed and beaten to death in a street in West Hollywood in 1977. She had a couple of movies, a Coppertone TV ad, and two small roles in TV shows *Starksy and Hutch* and *Wonder Woman* under her belt, but—smart, beautiful, tall, and blonde—she moved among A-listers on the LA party scene. She was reported to have kept audiotapes and a diary that rated her sexual encounters with Hollywood celebrities and rock stars—and so police suspected she might have been killed to hush her up. The tapes and diary had disappeared.

Born Sandra Wohlfeil in 1949 in Wisconsin, she married as a teenager and had a daughter, Nicole. Her husband disappeared right after, and she was told he had been killed in a Florida motorbike accident, but she was not convinced he had not just wanted to make himself scarce. Leaving Nicole with a friend, Wohlfeil moved to New York City to try to make it as a model. Intelligent, ambitious, determined, and good-looking, she began to make money and was welcomed onto the celebrity party circuit. Around this time, she changed her name to Christa Helm. She lived in a luxurious apartment, ran with the in-crowd, and was named "Bachelorette of the Month" in *Cosmopolitan*.

Helm secured minor roles in two movies, the horror film *Legacy of Satan*, filmed in 1972, and *Let's Go for Broke*, filmed the following year by Ron Walsh. In 1974 she moved to Hollywood and began to make her way in the TV industry, making a high-profile commercial. Very well connected from her New York City days, Helm had no trouble finding her feet and, soon after arriving, she began to stay with flamboyant financier Bernie Cornfeld in his vast mansion in Beverly Hills. In tune with the times, she even set to work on a disco album—but it was never released.

In this period on the LA scene Helm was romantically linked in the press with Hollywood and rock-music royalty. The story circulated that she was flown to the Shah of Iran's palace to entertain him, and there were rumors at this time that party girls, models, and actresses like Helm were secretly working for the US government to dig up facts about the Shah and Iran.

Below: Helm turned her fortunes around and "made it" in Hollywood—here she is in the hit show *Wonder Woman*.

Above: One report indicated that Helm had set out with a handbag that was missing from the scene of the attack—had it contained the audiotapes?

NIGHT ATTACK

On the night she died, Helm was due to go to a party in Hollywood and asked her agent Sandy Smith to go with her. When he declined, she drove across to his house to try to persuade him to come out. This was her final journey.

In front of the agent's house, Helm was ambushed from behind. Her attacker stabbed her 22 times, inflicting several wounds on her face and neck, and then battered her with a blunt object that may have been a hammer. She was found by a passerby, lying half underneath her car. She died shortly after the attack. Some say that the ferocity of the attack suggests that her assailant was someone who was angry with Helm; it does not look like a simple mugging.

There was soon speculation that Helm had been carrying the diary or audiotapes she was believed to have made. Some have commented that coverage of her death was surprisingly low-key, given that she was a regular name in gossip columns at the time, and speculate that the matter may have been hushed up by powerful people who wanted it kept quiet. A friend from Wisconsin, Darlene, reports that Helm sent her a postcard reading, "I am in way over my head here. I'm into something I can't get out of."

Helm's daughter, Nicole, has tried to uncover what happened and achieve justice for her mother, but it seems likely we will never know whether Christa Helm's death was the result of a random attack or part of a high-level conspiracy.

— STRANGE —
STORIES

Is it possible that Christa Helm was killed in a simple robbery that got out of hand? Initially, Hollywood police believed that there might be a connection between Christa Helm's death and that of strikingly handsome actor Sal Mineo, one of the stars of the iconic picture *Rebel Without a Cause*. There were spooky similarities. He was stabbed to death exactly one year earlier— February 12, 1976—in the same area. A pizza deliveryman, Lionel Williams, was convicted of Mineo's murder and several robberies, and was jailed until the 1990s. The attack on Mineo was believed to be a robbery rather than a personally motivated assault. In the end, the Helm–Mineo connection seemed to dissipate because it was understood that Lionel Williams was in jail at the time of Helm's murder. It has since been discovered that he was arrested for the Mineo murder *after* Helm was killed.

Above: Perhaps Helm had simply been the victim of a violent robbery by a pizza deliveryman, as had actor Sal Mineo.

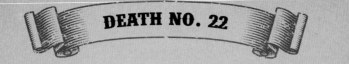

WAS BBC JOURNALIST JILL DANDO KILLED BY A HITMAN?

Date: April 26, 1999
Location: Fulham, West London, England

Jill Dando was gunned down on her doorstep in West London, some say by a professional killer working on the orders of Serbian dictator Slobodan Milošević.

This killing shocked the British nation. TV star Jill Dando, best known for presenting the BBC show *Crimewatch*, was shot dead with a single bullet to her head outside her home in Fulham, West London, at 11:30 a.m. on April 26, 1999. She was 37.

A local man named Barry George was convicted of her murder and sentenced to life imprisonment, but was cleared in 2008 after a retrial. Theories abound as to who ordered and executed the killing of the well-liked broadcaster and journalist—from crime bosses to hitmen working for Serbian warlords.

Born in Somerset, southwest England, Dando worked her way up through regional newspapers and TV, and was a presenter on news magazine show *Spotlight* in Devon before graduating to national news programs on the BBC, working on breakfast TV, the national news, the *Holiday* travel program, and the very popular *Crimewatch* series, which appealed for information to help the police close unsolved cases. She was voted BBC Personality of the Year in 1997.

On the day she was killed, Dando had left the house of her fiancé, gynecologist Alan Farthing, in Chiswick, London, and, after going shopping, went to her own house in nearby Fulham. Press reports

Above: The professional broadcaster—Dando presented *Crimewatch*, which undoubtedly would have gained her some enemies in the criminal underworld.

at the time indicated she was grabbed from behind on her own doorstep, then her head was forced to the ground, and she was shot through her left temple with a 9-mm semi-automatic pistol. The bullet went right through her head and came out the right side. She died instantly.

Her neighbor, Richard Hughes, reported he had heard Dando call out—"like someone greeting a friend," he said—but did not hear a gunshot. So he was not aware of what had happened when he looked out the window, but he did get the only eyewitness view of the presumed killer—according to Hughes, a white man, around 6 feet (1.83 meters) tall, and aged roughly 40.

Due to Dando's prominence, the case attracted major media attention, but the police made little progress, despite taking more than 1,000 statements and speaking to upward of 2,500 people. They then focused their attention on Barry George, a local man with Asperger's and a history of stalking and sex offences. He was arrested on May 25, 2000, over a year after the killing.

Above: Crowds pay their respects to the much loved and well respected presenter as the funeral cortège travels through Dando's hometown of Weston-super-Mare in 1999.

After his conviction and sentencing in 2001, George appealed twice without success. However, his third appeal was successful, as key forensics evidence had been discredited—the evidence had suggested that a gunshot particle found in his pocket was from the murder weapon, but the revisited evidence said it could have come from somewhere else. A retrial in 2008 found him not guilty of the offence.

SEX RING, CRIMINAL UNDERWORLD?

Was Jill Dando silenced because she planned to unveil a high-level sex offenders' ring operating within the BBC, where she worked? According to this line of thought, Dando had put together a dossier about pedophiles operating within the BBC and had handed it to senior management in the corporation. The BBC said there was no evidence of this. Several other theories were proposed and rejected. They included that the killing was a case of mistaken identity, that Dando was killed by a jealous former lover, or that she was tracked and slain by a stalker—an obsessed fan.

Many people suggested that the murder had the hallmark of a professional killing, and was more likely carried out by a trained hitman than by an ordinary member of the public like Barry George. They pointed to the fact that the killer or killers managed to get in and out almost entirely without being seen, and left no DNA or fingerprint evidence behind.

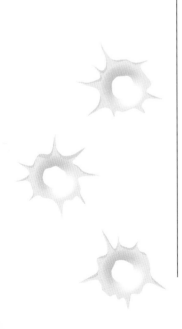

One prominent theory was that the hit was ordered by a member of the London criminal underworld. This theory proposes that the killing was ordered because Dando was a high-profile investigator of crime on TV. A similar but unlinked explanation was that an English barman resident in Tenerife and named "Joe" carried out the killing on behalf of an associate who had been jailed after a *Crimewatch* appeal.

SERBIAN ASSASSIN?

A widely proposed argument is that Dando was killed by a Serbian hitman, apparently as a revenge attack after she made a TV appeal for Kosovan refugees, who had been forced from their homes by Serbian militias. Some sources say it was ordered by Serbian dictator Slobodan Milošević himself. (Milošević was later charged with war crimes in Bosnia, Croatia, and Kosovo and tried before the International Criminal Tribunal for the Former Yugoslavia in the Hague. He died of a heart attack in his prison cell in 2006 and the unfinished trial was wound up without a verdict.)

Below: Could it be that the crime was a politically motivated act that can be traced back to Serbian dictator Slobodan Milošević?

Another idea was that it was revenge for a NATO-led bombing campaign that had hit a state-run TV station in Belgrade three days before, killing 16 people, including one of Milošević's close friends. At Barry George's original trial his defense barrister quoted from a National Criminal Intelligence Service report, stating that the Serbian warlord Arkan had ordered the murder as revenge for the NATO bombing.

The wife of a Serbian opposition journalist who was murdered in very similar circumstances to Jill Dando said in 2012 that she thought the British broadcaster and her husband had both been killed by hitmen working for Milošević. On April 11, 1999—15 days before Dando's death—the Serbian journalist Slavko Curuvija was forced to the ground and shot through the head on the doorstep of his home in Belgrade.

STRANGE STORIES

Was Dando's death an IRA killing? This theory—that the broadcaster was killed by a four-man squad acting on behalf of the Irish Republican Army—was based on a letter written from prison by a convicted killer who said Dando was targeted because of her connection through *Crimewatch* to police work. The letter writer claimed the killers shot Dando then escaped in a Land Rover to a London safehouse.

Above: A convicted killer claims that the case remains unsolved due to its links with the IRA, who targeted Jill Dando as a BBC journalist connected to police work.

He said this line of inquiry was closed down because the authorities did not want to jeopardize the ongoing peace process in Northern Ireland.

ACCIDENT, SUICIDE—OR MURDER?

Good detectives look closely at accidental deaths: Are they something more than they initially appear to be? Does identifying them as an accident cover up the fact that they were a suicide, or even a murder? In some notable deaths, inconvenient or unpleasant facts cast doubt on the "accidental" verdict. The second Norman king of England, William II, is said to have been shot by accident while hunting in the New Forest in 1100. While medieval hunting was certainly dangerous, the shooter was a highly skilled marksman who would surely not have taken a dangerous shot. What's more, William's brother, the future King Henry I, immediately had himself crowned,

Left: A life preserver marks the spot where Natalie Wood's body was found just off Blue Cavern Point on Catalina Island.

suggesting to some that the so-called accident was an assassination ordered by Henry. In 1959 George Reeves—famous as TV's Superman, but reputedly ambitious for movie roles and depressed at the way his career was going—is said to have shot himself in his bedroom in Los Angeles—but there are conflicting stories about what happened, even from those involved, and the ballistics evidence does not add up. Was he alone in the bedroom? Was his suicide a murder? Other Hollywood deaths—such as that of moviemaker and actor Thomas Ince, the "Father of the Western," and Natalie Wood, star of classic movies—seem to be more complicated than the accidents they appear to be at first. Indeed, some cases, such as Wood's, have been reopened and remain under scrutiny.

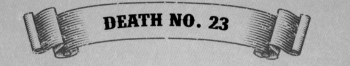

WAS KING WILLIAM II SHOT BY ACCIDENT—OR WAS IT MURDER?

Date: August 2, 1100
Location: New Forest, England

England's second Norman king—son of William the Conqueror—was shot with an arrow while out hunting in the New Forest. Was his brother, the future King Henry I, behind the "accident"?

William II had been King of England for a little under 13 years when he went hunting on a summer's day in 1100. Deep in the woods of the New Forest, probably near the Hampshire village of Brockenhurst, he was killed when an arrow loosed by nobleman Walter Tirel went through his lung. This may have been a terrible accident. Or was it murder, an assassination plotted by his ambitious younger brother, Henry, who took the throne as Henry I and would go on to rule for 35 years?

All the noblemen in the hunting party abandoned the king's body where it fell, and William's corpse was later found by a local peasant. While Walter Tirel fled to France, Henry rode to Winchester, where he took possession of the castle and the royal treasury, then hurried on to London and was crowned in Westminster Abbey on August 5, just three days after William's death.

A NOBLE LINEAGE

William II—known as Rufus—was the third of four sons of William the Conqueror, the Norman lord who led the famous Norman invasion of England in 1066 and seized the throne as William I. William Rufus's mother was Matilda of Flanders, Queen of England and Duchess of Normandy.

Above: William II was known as Rufus (from the Latin for "red"), perhaps because he had red hair when young, or maybe because he had a reddish complexion.

Left: William's brother Henry wasted no time, managing to get himself crowned in Westminster Abbey just three days after the tragic event— a haste which cast suspicion on the new king.

Below: Was Walter Tirel (seen here fleeing the scene) having a bad day with his aim, did he have a motive of his own, or was he acting under orders?

William Rufus's eldest brother, Robert Curthose, quarreled violently with his father and brothers in the 1070s. They were partially reconciled ca. 1080, and before William I died in 1087 he made Robert Duke of Normandy and William Rufus King of England. The second-eldest brother, Richard of Normandy, had been killed ca. 1069–75, curiously, in a hunting accident in the New Forest, the very fate that befell William Rufus. The fourth and youngest brother became Henry I.

It was normal practice under the feudal system for a dying king or lord to bequeath his inherited lands (in William I's case, Normandy) to his eldest son and his conquered territory (England) to a younger son. It caused trouble: several Norman lords wanted Normandy and England to have a single ruler, and, led by Bishop Odo of Bayeux, William I's half-brother and a veteran of the Battle of Hastings, they rose in revolt in 1088, seeking to put Robert Curthose on the English throne. William Rufus defeated them, and then in 1095 brutally put down a second rebellion led by Robert de Mowbray, Earl of Northumberland.

William Rufus also clashed with the leaders of the English Church, being unwilling to accept the Gregorian Reforms (named after Pope Gregory VII) promoted by Anselm, Archbishop of Canterbury. In 1097 William drove Anselm into exile and, after that date, kept the Archbishop's revenues for himself.

THE TURN OF EVENTS

The Church largely welcomed the demise of William Rufus. The monks who wrote contemporary chronicles largely saw it as an act of God, a fitting end for a wicked ruler who had behaved outrageously toward Archbishop Anselm.

Henry's response had been particularly swift and immediate—riding straight to Winchester, seizing the treasury, and being crowned. He hadn't even waited for Archbishop Thomas of York, who should have performed the coronation in the absence of Archbishop Anselm of Canterbury, but had himself crowned by Maurice of London, a mere bishop. Henry's haste might suggest the "accident" was a deliberate killing, a planned assassination that opened the way for the youngest brother to take power.

Below: The flight of Henry after William's death—did he have it all planned out in advance or was he just quick to react and make the most of an unfortunate (for William) turn of events?

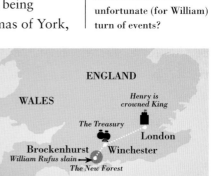

ENGLAND

WALES

Henry is crowned King

The Treasury

London

Brockenhurst   Winchester

William Rufus slain →

The New Forest

Some point out that Walter Tirel was known to be a skilled bowman and would be unlikely to take a risky or inept shot. Didn't his sudden flight to France, abandoning his former monarch's body on the forest floor, suggest he was guilty of killing him deliberately? Equally, though, he might have fled because he knew that it looked like he might have killed him deliberately— and so he made himself scarce.

On the other hand, some experts suggest that the timing of the incident indicates that it was, in fact, an accident. Noted historian John Gillingham argues that Henry did not eliminate William Rufus at this point and would have been better off waiting; the likelihood was that William Rufus and Robert Curthose, who were at loggerheads, would soon be at war—and one would then be taken out of the equation, meaning that Henry would be able to take control of England *and* Normandy with one killing.

Below: Hunting shy deer in a thick forest does sound like a dangerous sport, but perhaps not one in which you need fear being accidentally killed by a highly skilled marksman.

— STRANGE —
STORIES

Many historians accept the proposal that William Rufus's death was an accident. In those days hunting was very dangerous—William's own brother Richard of Normandy had been accidentally shot in a weirdly similar incident around a quarter of a century earlier. Not only that, but his nephew, another Richard, one of the illegitimate sons of Robert Curthose, was also shot by accident in the New Forest while hunting. One account of William Rufus's death indicates that Walter Tirel shot an arrow at a stag but it deflected off a tree and hit the king full in the chest, puncturing his lung and killing him. The well-known Rufus Stone, close to the village of Minstead in Hampshire, reputedly marks the spot where the tree stood. According to tradition, King Charles II visited the place and saw the tree in the seventeenth century, but the tree was later cut down and the stone was raised in the eighteenth century. King George III visited in 1789.

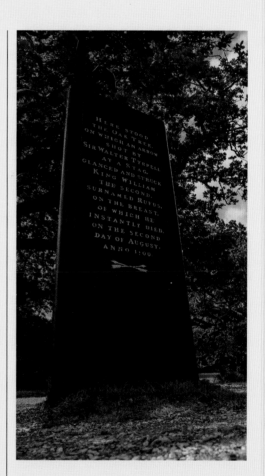

Above: The actual positioning of the Rufus Stone monument is dubious, but nevertheless, it serves as a memorial to a historic event.

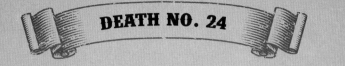

WAS MERIWETHER LEWIS MURDERED—OR DID HE KILL HIMSELF?

Date: October 11, 1809
Location: Old Natchez Trace forest trail, Tennessee

The explorer and veteran of the famous Lewis and Clark Expedition died a violent death at a remote inn—was it a robbery-murder or suicide?

In 1809 Meriwether Lewis set out for the nation's capital in Washington, D.C., to clear his name and justify his expenditure and actions as Governor of the Territory of Upper Louisiana. The former personal secretary of President Thomas Jefferson and captain of the pioneering Lewis and Clark Expedition, Lewis had seen his actions called into question, and he had suffered the indignity of his expense documents being rejected by William Eustis, Secretary of War.

Lewis was just 35. He had a successful military career before being appointed by Jefferson to lead the Lewis and Clark Expedition of 1804–06. His success in this venture, alongside his friend William

Clark, was followed by a grant of land and appointment by Jefferson in 1807 as Governor of Upper Louisiana. Lewis was delayed taking up the position and clashed with Louisiana territorial secretary Frederick Bates, as well as being criticized in D.C. for failing to keep his superiors well informed.

ISOLATED STOPOVER

On his fateful journey east in October 1809, Lewis left the Mississippi River at Chickasaw Bluffs in Tennessee and set out along the Old Natchez Trace forest trail, later stopping for the night at an inn called Grinder's Stand near modern Hohenwald, Tennessee. He was carrying several pistols, a rifle, and a tomahawk.

Above: The Lewis and Clark Expedition of 1804–06 was designed to explore the expanse of land in the western half of the Mississippi River basin and proceed into the Pacific Northwest.

After dinner he went to his cabin to sleep, then, in the hours before dawn, the innkeeper's wife, Priscilla Grinder, heard gunshots. Lewis's servants found him with several wounds, including one in the gut and one in the head. He bled to death, dying just after sunrise. This account was published in the *Democratic Clarion* newspaper in Nashville. According to the newspaper, Lewis's throat had been cut and money he had reputedly borrowed for the journey had been taken.

CONFLICTING ACCOUNTS

Priscilla Grinder never made a formal written testimony but reportedly gave several contradictory accounts of the events. In one version she said Lewis had been acting oddly the night before his death, his face flushed, pacing up and down and talking to himself. She later heard him talking to himself in his cabin, and heard a scuffle, gunshots, and the sound of someone crying for help. She said that, frightened by the commotion, she looked out through the crack in her door and saw Lewis crawling back toward his cabin.

Another account said the servants found Lewis with part of his skull blown away, but that he survived for several hours. A third version has it that Priscilla Grinder saw three men follow Lewis along the Old Natchez Trail and he drew his pistols on them; later she heard raised voices and gunshots in the cabin. His body was found outside the cabin, which had a significant amount of gunpowder on the floor.

Lewis's body was buried near the inn. Some, including Lewis's old friend and mentor, Thomas Jefferson, saw this is as a suicide, saying that Lewis was drinking heavily and depressed because he had not yet found a wife or published his three-volume account of the expedition. His former partner, William Clark, had previously seen Lewis in low spirits and, on hearing the news of his death, responded: "I fear the weight of his mind had overcome him." The twentieth-century historian Paul Russell Cutright suggested Lewis may have begun using opium or morphine, and might have been distressed by the decline in his long-standing relationship with Jefferson. Some say he may have had syphilis or malaria.

Others see the incident as an attack by thieves, an assassination by political rivals, or even an accident. It is difficult, though, to explain why he would have had so many wounds if they were inflicted accidentally.

Below: A replica cabin now stands in the place of the real one—exactly what happened inside the latter is unclear.

Right: Today, the Meriwether Lewis National Monument marks the site at which Lewis met his end.

─ STRANGE ─
STORIES

Murder most foul? In 1848, almost four decades after Lewis's unsolved death, his body was exhumed for analysis. The report of the Tennessee State Commission concluded that while many had presumed the explorer had taken his own life, it was more likely that he "died at the hands of an assassin." Much later again, in the years after 1993, a group of Lewis's descendants attempted to get official clearance to have his body exhumed so that forensic experts could determine whether he had killed himself or not. Although a coroner's jury gave its support, the National Park Service—who had authority because Lewis's grave lies on a national monument—did not allow it. Another attempt in 2008–10 was turned down by the Department of the Interior.

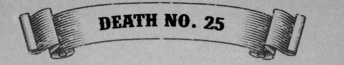

WAS THE "FATHER OF THE WESTERN" SHOT?

Date: November 19, 1924
Location: Los Angeles, California

Did pioneering moviemaker and actor Thomas H. Ince die of natural causes, or was he accidentally shot on board newspaper magnate William Randolph Hearst's luxury yacht?

Thomas Ince—the movie star, director, and pioneer producer known as the "Father of the Western"—was guest of honor aboard newspaperman William Randolph Hearst's 280-foot (85-meter) yacht, the *Oneida*, on November 16, 1924. The celebrity party was marking Ince's 44th birthday and a deal under which Hearst's Cosmopolitan Productions would use Ince's Hollywood studio for filming. Ince had to break up the social gathering: he was rushed ashore, reportedly suffering from severe indigestion, and died three days later, at home in Los Angeles, officially due to a heart attack.

On board the yacht at the time were global movie star Charlie Chaplin, British author and scriptwriter Elinor Glyn, actresses including Margaret Livingston and Julanne Johnston, and Hearst's mistress, the actress Marion Davies. Overheated rumors were soon circulating about what had happened. According to one, Hearst had caught Marion Davies and Charlie Chaplin in intimate relations and then shot Ince, having mistaken him for Chaplin.

Below: William Randolph Hearst (left) was a true media magnate, who, once his political career came to an end, had an open affair with actress Marion Davies (right).

THE RUMOR MILL

Chaplin's personal valet, Toraichi Kono, apparently saw Ince being carried ashore on a stretcher at San Diego and said he had a bullet wound in his head. This tidbit circulated among the Japanese domestic workers in Beverly Hills. What's more, the story goes that the morning edition of the *Los Angeles Times* for Wednesday, November 19, read "Movie Producer Shot on Hearst Yacht," but the headline had vanished by the time the evening edition came out. The Hearst-owned newspapers reported that Ince had been taken ill at Hearst's home, the famous San Simeon Castle. Other wild rumors suggested that Hearst had poisoned Ince, had him killed by a professional assassin, or even stabbed him with a hatpin in the heart.

Ince's body was cremated. Some later saw this as grist for the rumor mill, since the cremation meant the body could not be examined for evidence of bullet wounds or poison. Ince and his wife, Elinor, or "Nell," were committed Theosophists, members of an esoteric religious-philosophical group who believed in

Above: Hearst-owned newspapers reported that Ince was taken ill at San Simeon Castle—Hearst's mansion.

cremation among many other things, and had agreed long before his death that he should be cremated. There is also a story that Hearst set up a trust fund for Nell Ince and paid off the mortgage on a Los Angeles apartment she owned, but there was no truth in this, since Nell already owned the apartment in question before her husband's death, and would not have needed a trust fund because her husband's death left her an independently very wealthy woman.

The stories about Ince's death rather overshadowed his reputation for posterity, but he was a highly significant movie pioneer, responsible for more than 800 movies, including *Custer's Last Fight* (1912), *The Italian* (1915), and *Civilization* (1916), and for creating the first Hollywood studio—Inceville. He also developed the movie producer role.

Below: Was movie pioneer and producer Thomas H. Ince, here on set in 1923, and the director of many shootouts in Westerns, himself the victim of a shooting?

After Ince's death, another rumor circulated to the effect that Louella Parsons, later a celebrated movie columnist, was onboard the *Oneida* and that her rise to stardom—supported by Hearst, who gave her a lifetime contract to write for his newspapers—was driven by a deal she cut with Hearst to hush up the events on the yacht and Ince's death. This has been shown to be false, for she had been hired the year before by Hearst's *New York American* newspaper as motion picture editor.

A CASE OF ANGINA?

It seems we will never know for sure what happened on board the *Oneida*. The likeliest explanation seems to be that Ince did indeed fall ill and die of natural causes. Eyewitnesses, including Nell herself, reported this. Another pointer is that the *Los Angeles Times* reported that at Ince's memorial service, his casket was open for an hour to give friends and loved ones the chance to say their farewells—and not one mentioned any sign of a bullet wound. Nell said Ince needed treatment for very bad chest pains resulting from angina, while the couple's son William, who later became a practicing medic, said he thought Ince's illness seemed like thrombosis. According to Adela Rogers St. Johns, a writer and friend of the Inces, Nell later said, "Do you think I would have done nothing if I even suspected that my husband had been victim of foul play?"

Above: Having unwittingly played its part in an enduring scandal of Hollywood-movie proportions, the *Oneida* was sold by Hearst after 1927 and was then used as a ferry on Lake Champlain.

— STRANGE —
STORIES

The stories about Ince's death have been given new life by fictional treatments. Hearst's granddaughter Patricia Hearst published, with coauthor Cordelia Frances Biddle, a 1996 mystery novel, *Murder at San Simeon*, that cast Charlie Chaplin and Marion Hearst as lovers and Hearst as a jealous older man. Then in 2001 revered director Peter Bogdanovich made *The Cat's Meow*, a dramatization of the events on board the *Oneida*. In this movie, Hearst mistakenly shoots Ince, thinking he is Chaplin, when he finds him sitting talking with Davies; Hearst has the dying Ince taken off the boat at San Diego. Another part of the Ince myth is played out in the movie: Louella Parsons witnesses the event and trades her silence for a lifetime contract as a gossip columnist for Hearst's newspapers. Hearst is played by Edward Herrmann, Davies by Kirsten Dunst, Ince by Cary Elwes, and Parsons by Jennifer Tilly. Bogdanovich did not write the screenplay, which was by playwright Steven Peros, but in

publicity about the movie it was reported he had gotten the lowdown on what happened on board the yacht from no less a figure than moviemaker Orson Welles, who had heard it from screenwriter Charles Lederer, nephew of Marion Davies herself.

Below: Could it be that the great Charlie Chaplin had dared to cross Hearst by having an affair with Marion?

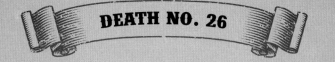

DID SUPERMAN KILL HIMSELF?

Date: June 16, 1959
Location: Los Angeles, California

Some say TV *Superman* actor George Reeves was shot by a hitman or accidentally killed by his fiancée, but the official line was that he took his own life.

Actor George Reeves—star of hit 1950s TV show *Adventures of Superman*—was found dead in his bedroom at home in Benedict Canyon, Los Angeles, on June 16, 1959, having apparently shot himself in the head. While the official verdict was suicide, rival theories suggest he was shot by his fiancée, Leonore Lemmon, or was killed by a professional hitman, hired by studio executive Eddie Mannix or his wife, Toni. Toni had been having an affair with the victim.

Reeves got off to a good start in his acting career, being cast in a minor role as a suitor of the heroine Scarlett O'Hara in the classic *Gone with the Wind* in his first year in the industry, and then making films with stars like Ronald Reagan and Jimmy Cagney under contract to Warner Brothers. Work slowed down

for Reeves after World War II, although he continued to land minor roles alongside major stars in big films—with Marlene Dietrich in the Fritz Lang Western *Rancho Notorious* in 1952 and with Burt Lancaster and Frank Sinatra in *From Here to Eternity* in 1953. By then he had been cast as Superman on TV.

The TV show *Adventures of Superman* made Reeves a national celebrity—much to his surprise. He had been reluctant to take the part, thinking TV a sidetrack to the main road of his career, in the movies. And, despite its success, he felt constrained by it. Tight contracts to ensure cast and crew were ready to film a new series of the TV show at short notice meant that it was virtually impossible to take on movie or theater work. In 1954 he tried and failed to get his own TV production company and series—a

Above: In 1959 Reeves hooked up with wealthy socialite Leonore Lemmon, who was present on the night of his death. The couple are pictured here at Coconut Grove Playhouse, Miami, 1959.

venture called *Port of Entry*—off the ground. According to his friend Ben Welden, Reeves felt trapped by the Superman role and said, "Here I am, wasting my life."

ROMANCE SOURED

The background to the events of June 16, 1959, is that Reeves split from his long-term mistress, Toni Mannix, and took up with wealthy socialite Leonore Lemmon. He had been seeing Mannix since as early as 1951. On the day he died, he was drinking and socializing with Lemmon and a friend, the writer Robert Condon; Lemmon and Reeves argued in a restaurant before returning home with Condon in tow to continue the party. An alternative version, told by Lemmon, is that the three of them went to a wrestling bout that evening rather than a restaurant.

Above: Did Reeves's long-term mistress, Toni Mannix, arrange to have him killed?

Left: Reeves felt limited by the role of Superman—despite its success—but did he feel so trapped that he wanted to end his own life?

At home in Benedict Canyon, Reeves went to bed while the other two stayed up drinking and talking. Around midnight, neighbors Bill Bliss and Carol Van Ronkel arrived, and the party got a new lease of life. Reeves came downstairs to complain about the noise, but stayed for a drink before returning to bed. Then a gunshot rang out.

CONFUSION—AND CONTRADICTORY EVIDENCE

When the police were called, they found the guests to be drunk and their accounts of what had happened confusing. According to the most commonly told version, Bliss ran upstairs and found Reeves lying back on the bed with a Luger pistol on the floor— in a position consistent with his having shot himself in the head while sitting on the bed's edge. Press reports suggested Reeves was depressed because he felt stuck playing Superman and could not get the movie roles that he wanted. Rumors and later accounts suggested that Lemmon might have been in the room with Reeves, or just outside the bedroom, when the fatal shot was fired.

Above: A Luger pistol was reportedly found lying next to Reeves on the bed, but the associated gunpowder, bullets, and fingerprints (or lack thereof) have caused confusion.

Several puzzling pieces of evidence seem to cast doubt on the accepted version of events: there was no gunpowder residue on Reeves's hands, as there would have been if he had used the gun, and his fingerprints were not found on the gun—in fact, no fingerprints were found, as if it had been wiped. While the bullet that killed Reeves and passed through his body was found in the ceiling, its casing was found beneath his body, as if he had been moved. Two other bullets fired from the same gun were found in the floor, but all the witnesses said only one shot had been fired. There was no evidence at all that a second person had been in the room with him, and no sign of anyone breaking into the house or the room.

Was it a suicide? Reeves's mother hired an attorney to press for the case to be reopened as a homicide, but he did not find any definitive evidence, and later accepted the suicide explanation. Rory Calhoun, a fellow actor, veteran of many Westerns, and friend of Reeves, reportedly said that "no one in Hollywood believed the suicide story." One theory is that Leonore Lemmon accidentally killed her fiancé while in the room with him and the gun. Another is that Toni Mannix, maddened by his rejection of her, had him killed or shot him herself, while a third is that her husband Eddie Mannix, who allegedly had underworld connections, arranged a hit on Reeves, and took Superman down.

— STRANGE —
STORIES

Above: The movie version of the events, *Hollywoodland*, starred Diane Lane (left) as Toni Mannix, seen here with Jeffrey DeMunn as Reeves's manager, Art Weissman. Ben Affleck portrayed Reeves.

In 1999, LA publicist Edward Lozzi made the claim that Toni Mannix had confessed to a Roman Catholic priest in his presence that she had arranged for Reeves to be killed. Mannix had died in 1983 after suffering from Alzheimer's disease for many years and Lozzi knew her in 1979–82. He claimed she made the confession while in a period of mental lucidity before she had to move from her home to be cared for in a hospital.

In 2006 the movie *Hollywoodland*, directed by Allen Coulter, dramatized the events surrounding Reeves's death, but allowed room for any of the three main explanations of events—suicide, an accidental shooting by Leonore Lemmon, or a hit arranged by Eddie or Toni Mannix—to be true.

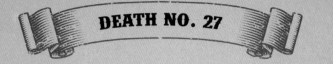
WAS JIMI HENDRIX MURDERED?

Date: September 18, 1970
Location: Notting Hill, London, England

Did Jimi Hendrix's manager Michael Jeffery order the killing of one of rock music's greatest guitarists—or did Jimi die, as officially stated, in a tragic accident after mixing red wine and barbiturates?

Rock-music fans were stunned when American guitarist Jimi Hendrix—one of the great heroes of the fabled Woodstock Music Festival in August 1969—died suddenly, aged just 27, in September 1970. The official verdict was that he died from asphyxiation after inhaling his own vomit, having taken barbiturates and drunk a huge amount of red wine. In the years since, rumors have swirled around this tragic death, some suggesting suicide, others an FBI hit, others that his manager was behind a plot to kill the singer-guitarist.

Born in Seattle, Washington, in 1942, Hendrix began playing guitar and formed a band in his mid-teens, then in 1961 joined the US Army. He completed paratrooper training but was granted an honorable discharge on the grounds of unsuitability. Hendrix made his way as a musician in Nashville, Tennessee, and then Harlem, New York, and went on tour as a guitarist with the Isley Brothers and Little Richard, before going to London.

Hendrix soon won the stunned admiration of his fans and peers, famously setting his guitar on fire after a performance at the London Astoria, and releasing the singles "Hey Joe" and "Purple Haze." Back in the US, he made an iconic performance of "The Star Spangled Banner" on electric guitar at Woodstock in 1969. By this stage, his band, the Experience, had split up.

Below: Hendrix was a phenomenal hit, playing with all the big stars of the time and with his own band, the Jimi Hendrix Experience, as well as performing on the festival circuit.

FINAL HOURS

In the fall of 1970, Hendrix's European tour with a new band lineup was not going well. Some say he was paranoid, and he reportedly talked to friends about leaving his manager, Jeffery.

On September 18, according to the widely accepted version, Hendrix was picked up from a friend's in the night by his girlfriend, Monika Dannemann, who then took him home to her Notting Hill apartment. They stayed up talking until 7 a.m., then slept. When Dannemann woke at 11 a.m., Hendrix was still breathing but did not respond to her. She called an ambulance, but he lost consciousness on the way to the hospital, and was declared dead at 12:45 p.m. An autopsy found that Hendrix had choked on his vomit after drinking wine and taking barbiturates, and an inquest delivered an open verdict.

Another version is that Hendrix was already dead when the ambulance crew arrived at the apartment. Some accounts have it that he had taken nine sleeping pills—18 times the recommended dose. Other reports indicate that there were vast amounts of wine in his stomach and lungs, and his hair was soaked in wine, but his blood alcohol level was low, and so either he drank it quickly or he was effectively drowned in wine. One theory is that the FBI killed Hendrix as part of a counterintelligence program aimed at stamping out subversive influences. The line of argument is that his manager, Michael Jeffery, had underworld connections.

Michael Jeffery died in 1973 following a midair collision between two airliners in France, and Dannemann was found dead in 1996, having apparently committed suicide. Whatever really happened, the events in that Notting Hill room in September 1970 robbed the music world of a true guitar great.

Above: Hendrix's girlfriend, Monika Dannemann, woke up next to an unresponsive Hendrix.

— STRANGE —
STORIES

Did Michael Jeffery arrange for Hendrix to be killed, so he could get rich on the rock-star's royalties? This is the theory put forward by one of Hendrix's former roadies, James "Tappy" Wright, in a 2009 book, *Rock Roadie*. Jeffery was in Spain at the time of Hendrix's death but, according to Wright, he hired a gang who broke into Dannemann's flat and forced painkillers and wine down Hendrix's throat until he was drowned. Wright even says that Jeffery confessed to him before he died in 1973 that he had arranged the killing. He said that Jeffery was concerned about Hendrix's escalating drug-taking and had taken out a $2 million life insurance policy on the rock-star's life in Jeffery's name—he reputedly said Hendrix was "worth more to him dead than alive." Others point out that Hendrix had spoken with record producers Alan Douglas and Chas Chandler about finding a new manager to direct his career. If Jeffery was planning a hit, this news would have made the need more urgent.

Above: 22 Lansdowne Crescent in London is the house where Jimi Hendrix died, but how he died is less certain.

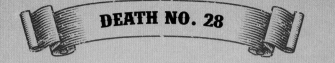

HOW DID NATALIE WOOD REALLY DIE?

Date: November 29, 1981
Location: Santa Catalina Island, California

The movie star was found drowned after being declared missing from husband Robert Wagner's yacht. Was this a tragic accident, or was foul play involved?

Hollywood A-listers Natalie Wood and Robert Wagner's Thanksgiving celebrations ended in tragedy and sparked a media frenzy in 1981, when Wood apparently drowned after falling from the couple's 60-foot (18-meter) yacht, the *Splendour*, off Santa Catalina Island.

Wood was a child star, in *Miracle on 34th Street* (1947), who became a major movie star and sparkled in a string of iconic films, including *Rebel Without a Cause*. The handsome Wagner was a successful star in the movies and a huge hit on TV. They were twice married, in 1957–62 and from 1972 to her death. In between they were romantically linked to an A-list of A-listers: Wood with Elvis Presley, Warren Beatty, Steve McQueen, and Frank Sinatra; Wagner with Elizabeth Taylor, Joan Crawford, and Anita Ekberg.

Right: Wood and Wagner—here starring in *All the Fine Young Cannibals* (1960)—were among the most beautiful of the "beautiful people."

THANKSGIVING TRAGEDY

Wood and Wagner were on vacation for Thanksgiving 1981 with Christopher Walken, with whom Wood was then filming *Brainstorm*. Wood disappeared after dining with Wagner, Walken, and the boat's captain, Dennis Davern, and was found face-down in the sea, wearing just her nightgown and socks, at 8 a.m. the next morning, approximately 1 mile (1.6 kilometers) away from the yacht, off Blue Cavern Point. Her body was bruised and her left cheek was grazed.

The autopsy found that she had a blood alcohol content of 0.14 percent, and had taken both a painkiller and a motion-sickness pill, which would have increased the physical effects of the alcohol. The LA County coroner ruled the death an accident, caused by hypothermia and drowning.

DRINKING AND ARGUMENTS

The reported sequence of events was that the four people had a champagne dinner onshore on the evening of November 28 and then returned to the yacht to continue drinking. Wood left the party at 10:45 p.m. and when Wagner went to bed he found she was not there. He phoned the authorities at 1:30 a.m.

It is believed that Wood tried to prevent the yacht bumping into a dinghy and fell overboard, then bruised and injured herself trying to clamber aboard the dinghy, finally drowning in the night-time Pacific Ocean. She had been brought face to face with her greatest fear—she had said, "I've always been terrified of water, of dark water, of sea water."

In his 2008 memoir, Wagner wrote that after returning to the yacht he and Walken began arguing. He said either Wood was trying to find somewhere to get away from the noisy row or she was trying to secure the dinghy. She must have fallen overboard, he said.

Below: Wagner and Walken argued on board the yacht *Splendour*. Had the relationship between Wood and Wagner turned sour, and was Walken to blame for this?

With champagne dinners, rowing superstars, and enduring mystery, the case has continued to fascinate movie fans for more than four decades. We likely have to accept that we will never know for sure how Wood met her end. It remains true, as Wagner wrote, that "the bottom line is that nobody knows exactly what happened."

— STRANGE —
STORIES

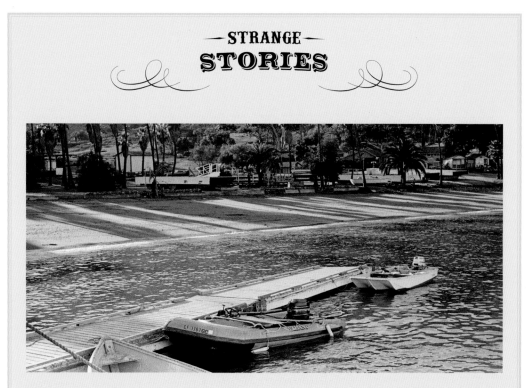

The case was reopened in 2011 when yacht captain Dennis Davern said he had lied in the original investigation and claimed that Wood and Wagner argued on the night of her death—he said that Wagner was angry to see Wood flirting with Walken. In 2012 the LA County chief coroner amended Wood's death certificate from accidental drowning to "drowning and other undetermined factors" and an associated statement said that how she ended up in the water was "not clearly established." The following year the coroner's office

Above: A dinghy was discovered near to Wood's floating, bruised body. Had it caused her death?

issued an addendum, which stated that she might have gotten some of the bruises on her body before she fell in the water, but this could not be determined. In 2018, now aged 87, Robert Wagner was named a "person of interest" in Wood's death by the LA County sheriff's department on CBS TV. The actor denied any involvement in her death and stated that he was not a suspect.

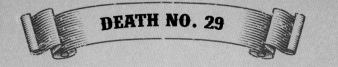

DID BOLLYWOOD ACTRESS DIVYA BHARTI JUMP—OR WAS SHE PUSHED?

Date: April 5, 1993
Location: Mumbai, India

This beautiful and hugely talented rising star of early 1990s Bollywood fell—or was pushed—from a Mumbai balcony, and tragically died from the resulting head injuries.

Bollywood actress Divya Bharti was near the top of the movie game—and still on the way up. Aged just 19, she had already starred in a string of hit movies, including the 1992 movie *Deewana*, which won her a best female debut award, and *Shola Aur Shabnam*. The young actress had signed up for several more roles and was halfway through the filming of *Laadla* when her life came to an untimely and violent end.

Born in Mumbai, Bharti had a huge hit with her first feature at the age of 16, the Telugu-language movie *Bobbili Raja*, which was followed by several more big Telugu hits before her first Bollywood

Right: Bharti had so much to live for. With a string of movie hits behind her, she was well established in Bollywood.

picture, *Vishwatma*, released in 1992. The song "Saat Samundar" in this movie made her a big star. The movie *Dil Ka Kya Kasoor* crashed, but her next movie, *Shola Aur Shabnam*, was a hit.

Bharti was married on May 10, 1992, to producer and director Sajid Nadiadwala, whom she had met through her leading man, Govinda, on *Shola Aur Shabnam*. Within a year she was dead.

On the night in question, she was with her maid, Amrita, and her friend and dress designer, Neeta Lulla, as well as Lulla's husband, a psychiatrist named Shyam Lulla. Neeta Lulla was there to discuss costumes for the upcoming movie *Andolan*. That day, Bharti had finalized arrangements for buying a large, four-room apartment in the reputable Bandra suburb of western Mumbai. She was in good spirits and had spoken animatedly with her brother Kunal about the new apartment. Recently returned from a shoot in Chennai, she was due to fly out for another shoot in Hyderabad, but was hoping to postpone her departure so that she could view her new flat. She was reportedly wearing a bandage on her left foot.

PRANK GONE WRONG?

The received narrative of what happened is that the group sat around with a couple of bottles of liquor. Neeta and Shyam Lulla were engrossed in watching a movie. Amrita went to the kitchen to prepare some food while she and Bharti carried on talking. In these few minutes, Bharti climbed out of the fifth-floor window and onto a narrow ledge; the window did not have a balcony or a grill to prevent people clambering out. Was she fooling around? Some people say that she loved to carry out pranks of this sort. If so, this one went gravely wrong. Bharti appears to have slipped off the narrow ledge and fallen five floors to the ground below. Twisting to try to save herself by catching hold of the window frame, she apparently fell down in such a way that she landed on her back and banged her head heavily. She was discovered in a pool of blood on the concrete beneath the window. She died at Cooper Hospital, Mumbai, from the head injuries.

Some 500 people, including movie greats such as Anil Kapoor, Govinda, and Raj Babbar, attended her funeral on April 7, 1993.

The police reportedly interviewed Shyam and Neeta Lulla, Amrita, Sajid Nadiadwala, Bharti's mother and father, and her brother. Amrita, who had looked after Bharti since she was a little girl, outlived her by less than a month. She died from a heart attack in May 1993. Mystery surrounds the star's fall. The police case was not closed until 1998; the official verdict is accidental death.

Above: Apparently the group had been drinking Black Label whiskey and Mauritian rum.

— STRANGE —
STORIES

Bharti's death at age 19—and with a glittering career stretching out before her—seemed so cruel, so inexplicable, that conspiracy theories soon swirled around it. One was that she committed suicide. She had a difficult relationship with her mother, the story goes, and on top of that had discovered that her husband had links to the underworld: emotionally disturbed, not thinking clearly, she threw herself from the window. There were rumors that she

Above: Bharti died from head injuries sustained when she tumbled from a fifth-floor window at the Tulsi Apartments in the Versova area of Mumbai, but why had she fallen?

had twice before tried to take her own life. Her nature was impulsive and her behavior unpredictable. Another wild theory was that her husband planned her murder. A third was that she was a little, or more than a little, drunk, and lost her balance for that reason.

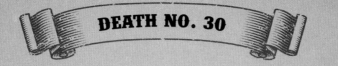

WAS RODNEY MARKS' DEATH THE FIRST MURDER AT THE SOUTH POLE?

Date: May 12, 2000
Location: Amundsen–Scott South Pole Station, Antarctica

The Australian astrophysicist died of methanol poisoning while working at the Amundsen–Scott South Pole Station, but no one has ever worked out precisely how or why.

R odney Marks' mysterious death was described in the media as possibly the "first South Pole murder." His death was initially described as being from natural causes, but after it emerged he had been poisoned with methanol, people began to talk of suicide, and possibly even murder. The case has never been solved.

Marks was working for the Smithsonian Astrophysical Observatory at the Antarctic Submillimeter Telescope and Remote Observatory at the Amundsen–Scott South Pole Station, run by the US government's National Science Foundation (NSF). It was a dream job for this youthful graduate of the University of

Melbourne, who had completed his PhD at the University of New South Wales. However, Marks suddenly fell ill on May 11, 2000, while walking from the observatory to the main base. Over the next 36 hours he felt worse and worse, and went back three times to the station medic, Robert Thompson, for help. He died on May 12 of unknown causes, aged just 32.

DELAYED AUTOPSY

The NSF initially stated that he had "apparently died of natural causes," but the specific cause of death was "yet to be determined." Winter conditions in Antarctica meant that his body had to be kept onsite until it could be flown to New Zealand for an autopsy. A postmortem in Christchurch reported that he had died from methanol poisoning. The New Zealand police began an investigation.

Above: Marks fell ill on his way to the main building, pictured here. He would seek medical attention three times.

The various pieces of evidence that emerged brought little clarity. Marks' body apparently had needle entry marks on the arms yet there were no illegal drugs in his system. Marks had Tourette syndrome, a neuropsychiatric disorder that manifests in verbal tics and muscular spasms. He was known to be a heavy drinker, partly because he saw this as a means of managing the condition. One suggestion was that he was attempting to distil his own spirits and had accidentally drunk the methanol. However, the base had a well-stocked bar that hardly ever closed, so Marks would have had no trouble in accessing alcoholic drinks if he wanted them, and he was a highly trained and skilled scientist, so the chances of his messing up to the extent of ingesting a poisonous substance—like methanol—in error must have been very low.

WAS MARKS SUICIDAL?

Another possibility was suicide. Perhaps feeling lonely, and given the isolation of the Antarctic with the winter setting in, and perhaps not quite in his right mind from drinking alcohol, had Marks deliberately ingested the methanol, knowing it would kill him? This seems unlikely when he had returned to the medic on three occasions, and those involved agreed that he had not seemed to be feigning his apparent panic; if he had taken poison and then regretted it, he could have explained the situation to the medic—but he had not. Moreover, Marks was not in a bad way: he had recently embarked on a romantic relationship with a young woman, who was working at the base so that they could be together. He was also close to completing some significant academic work, and he did not have any known financial or health worries.

Above: Did dark things happen in the isolated Dark Sector, where Marks was working on the night he became ill?

Right: The Amundsen–Scott South Pole Station is the southernmost habitation on Earth. The area map traces Marks' last movements.

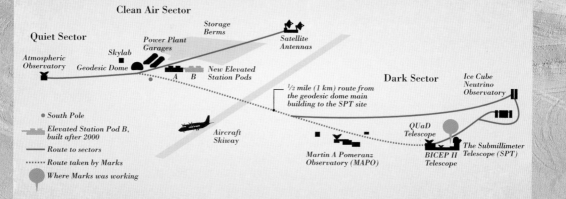

AREA MAP OF THE AMUNDSEN–SCOTT SOUTH POLE STATION

Clean Air Sector

Quiet Sector

Storage Berms

Satellite Antennas

Power Plant Garages

Skylab

Atmospheric Observatory

Geodesic Dome

A   B

New Elevated Station Pods

Dark Sector

Ice Cube Neutrino Observatory

½ mile (1 km) route from the geodesic dome main building to the SPT site

QUaD Telescope

The Submillimeter Telescope (SPT)

Aircraft Skiway

Martin A Pomeranz Observatory (MAPO)

BICEP II Telescope

- ● South Pole
- ▬ Elevated Station Pod B, built after 2000
- ▬ Route to sectors
- ⋯ Route taken by Marks
- ● Where Marks was working

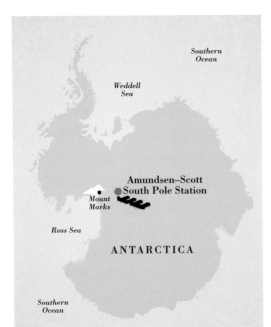

Above: Marks is
commemorated with a
plaque at the South Pole
and in the name of the
8,530-foot (2,600-meter)
Mount Marks in the
Worcester Range
in Antarctica.

WAS MARKS MURDERED?

Detective Senior Sergeant Grant Wormald
of the New Zealand police, in charge of
the investigation, found his efforts to elicit
further information from the NSF did not
go well. The NSF position was that the
death was from natural causes. When
Wormald asked to see an internal NSF
report he believed existed, he was told
there were no reports that were relevant
and the inquiries that had taken place
in the agency would be "of little value"
to him.

Jurisdiction over the base was not simple.
The remote observatory where Marks
worked was a project of the University of
Chicago, while Amundsen–Scott Station was run by the NSF, but
these were within the Ross Dependency, a section of Antarctica
claimed by New Zealand. The US does not recognize the New
Zealand claim or the application of New Zealand law to US
citizens within the area. So, there was little Wormald could do
to progress the matter.

In the end it seems unlikely the mystery around Marks' death
will ever be solved. The Christchurch coroner found in December
2006 that there was no evidence of murder, suicide, or of a prank
that had gone wrong. Wormald said that while Marks might
have taken the methanol for "recreational effect," he thought
this unlikely, and believed the likeliest scenario to be that
the astrophysicist had ingested the methanol "unknowingly."
Somehow Marks ingested the methanol that killed him, but
we will never know how or why.

— STRANGE —
STORIES

Another possible Antarctic poisoning case came to light in 2002. Edgar Evans, a member of British explorer Robert Falcon Scott's ill-fated *Terra Nova* expedition, died on February 17, 1912, during the party's return from the South Pole. It was thought that he injured his head in a fall into a crevasse on the Beardmore Glacier and went into a swift decline. However, in 2002 scientists discovered anthrax in the

Above: Anthrax was presumably carried from Asia, where it was endemic, by the mules and ponies the expedition brought with it.

stables at Scott's base camp at Cape Evans. The symptoms of Evans' decline, including mental confusion and extreme tiredness, are consistent with anthrax poisoning, and scientists suggest this may have been the cause.

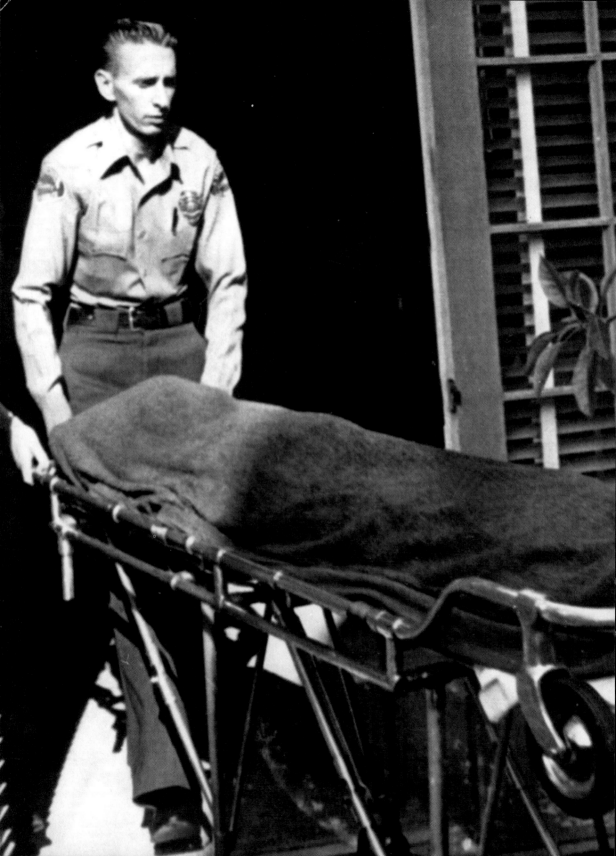

CONSPIRACY KILLINGS?

Some deaths seem to beg the question: Was there more to this than meets the eye? The reported facts of the case are confused, or the official verdict seems unconvincing. Often, victims are struck down in their prime, with shocking suddenness. Why? Who could have wanted this? In these circumstances, conspiracy theories are born and multiply—and the more famous the victim, the more convoluted and multitudinous the theories. Probably the most famous example, covered in other books in this series, is the shooting of US President John F. Kennedy in Dallas in 1963, but what of the death of JFK's reputed mistress Marilyn Monroe, who died in bed from acute barbiturate poisoning? Was this the work of the CIA? The Mafia? We also look at the untimely deaths of Pope John Paul I, just 33 days after his election to the papacy in 1978, and of kung fu movie star Bruce Lee, just as he was breaking into global stardom, in 1973—and at the many conspiracy theories surrounding these events. Conspiracy killings are not just a modern phenomenon: the disappearance of the Princes in the Tower (King Edward V and Richard, 1st Duke of York) has also inspired theories of a cover-up. Were the young princes murdered by their uncle to clear the way to his taking the crown as Richard III? We will likely never know for sure, but the conspiracy theories continue to swirl.

Left: Theories abound about the reasons for the death of Marilyn Monroe, cut down in her prime, with many high-powered and dubious connections.

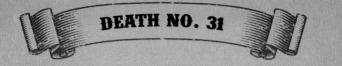

WAS EDWARD II MURDERED IN BERKELEY CASTLE—OR DID HE ESCAPE?

Date: September 21, 1327
Location: Berkeley Castle, Gloucestershire, England

Traditional accounts report that Edward II of England was killed in Berkeley Castle, but some historians say he escaped to live abroad and that the body of a porter or gatekeeper was buried in his place, as part of a royal conspiracy.

King Edward II of England was jailed at Berkeley Castle, Gloucestershire, after his estranged queen, Isabella, and her lover, Roger Mortimer, Earl of March, brought about his abdication on January 21, 1327. Edward was replaced on the throne by his son, who became Edward III. Poor judgment and self-indulgence had brought Edward II to ruin. He came to the throne in 1307, son of the great King Edward I, with good looks, bravery, and sharp wits on his side. He seemed destined for greatness himself, but he alienated his barons, and the queen.

OUTRAGE AND WRATH

Even before becoming king, Edward had embarked on a disastrous intimate relationship with Piers Gaveston, son of a Gascon knight and probably young Edward's lover. The king, Edward I, was outraged and banished Gaveston; but, on acceding to the throne himself, Edward II recalled his friend and made him Earl of Cornwall. He later married Gaveston to his niece Margaret, daughter of the Earl of Gloucester, Gilbert de Clare, and even made him regent when he himself went abroad to marry Isabella, daughter of King Philip IV "the Fair" of France. The leading barons turned on the King. Edward briefly gave in to their demands, sending Gaveston to Ireland, but then recalled him. On the favorite's return, the nobles seized and beheaded Gaveston at Blacklow Hill in Warwickshire, in June 1312.

Below: Edward in close conversation with his friend, and probable lover, Piers Gaveston—the real reason behind Edward's death?

By this time, Edward's relations with his queen had improved a little, and later that year she gave birth to a son, the future Edward III. Otherwise, things went from bad to worse: Edward led the English army to a humiliating defeat by Scottish King Robert I "the Bruce" at the famous Battle of Bannockburn in 1314 and, back in England, was sidelined by the Earl of Lancaster, who made himself effective ruler of the country.

Edward found new favorites in Hugh le Despenser and his father, of the same name, both from the Welsh Marches. Civil war erupted in 1321 as Lancaster banished the Despensers, but Edward won the Battle of Boroughbridge in Yorkshire the following year and had Lancaster executed. The Despensers returned, and Edward enjoyed an intense intimacy with Hugh le Despenser the Younger.

Below: Gaveston's head was the first to roll and is shown here to the Earl of Lancaster.

Above: Was Berkeley Castle the site of Edward's humiliation and torture, or did he manage to flee?

THE SHE-WOLF QUEEN

The final struggle began when Queen Isabella left for France and lived there openly with Mortimer. In England they called her "the she-wolf of France." The pair invaded in 1326 and Edward took flight to Wales. He was captured with Hugh the Younger in Caerphilly, Wales, on November 16. Hugh was executed and Edward held in captivity, initially in Monmouth, then in Kenilworth, Leicestershire, where he was finally persuaded to abdicate, so long as his son was given the throne. Edward III was crowned in Westminster Abbey on February 1, 1327, and Edward was moved to Berkeley Castle.

It was here that a royal conspiracy may have begun. Edward III was told on September 23 that his father had died in the night two days earlier, on September 21. The traditional account is gruesome: it is said that the former king's jailors wanted to humiliate him on account of the gossip about his sexual relationships with Gaveston and Hugh le Despenser the Younger; they supposedly inserted a metal funnel into his anus and then thrust a red-hot soldering iron into his bowels. He would have died in agony.

COVER-UP?

Most historians now reject this account. Some say Edward died of natural causes; others believe that he was killed but in a less brutal fashion. Some argue that the king was allowed to leave the country in secret and that he took off for continental Europe. The body of a porter who died in Berkeley Castle was presented by Isabella as that of the king and it was buried in his place.

There is one story that in 1338, while Edward III was in Koblenz, Germany, he met a man named William the Welshman, who said he was the former king. Another account (see box, opposite) tells that Edward III received a letter from a papal notary by the name of Manuele Fieschi, who said that Edward II made a daring escape from captivity and eventually settled to live in humble circumstances, more or less as a religious hermit, somewhere in the Holy Roman Empire.

Right: It may have been the case that Edward fled his captors and even managed to live out his days as a hermit—a more palatable version of events than his brutal death at the hands of his torturers.

— STRANGE —
STORIES

The "Fieschi Letter" that contains the supposed account of Edward II's escape to continental Europe was found in the French city of Montpellier in 1878; it was reputedly sent to Edward III ca. 1337. It says that Edward, on hearing that he was going to be put to death at Berkeley Castle, swapped clothing with a manservant, made his way in secret to the castle gate, killed the gatekeeper, and got away. He escaped to Corfe Castle in Dorset, southern England, and remained in hiding there for a whole 18 months, before fleeing to Ireland. After nine months there he reputedly traveled in disguise to the Low Countries and went on southward. He visited the Pope, possibly John XII, at Avignon—at this time the papacy was based in that French city rather than in Rome. After that, Edward is said to have settled to live as a hermit at Cecima near Pavia in Lombardy—perhaps at the abbey of Sant'Alberto di Butrio. There is a tradition at Cecima that an English King

Above: Did Edward live as a hermit at this abbey, Sant'Alberto di Butrio, in Pavia, Italy?

once lived there, and an empty tomb is said to have been that of Edward before his son had his body taken back to England. The letter is a genuine fourteenth-century document, not a later forgery, and Fieschi was a real person. Some say its contents are genuine; others that they were fabricated.

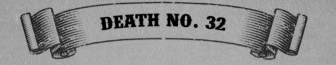

WERE THE "PRINCES IN THE TOWER" MURDERED AND WAS IT COVERED UP?

Date: 1483
Location: Tower of London, England

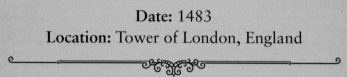

Edward V and his brother Richard were never seen again after being lodged, supposedly for their own safety, in the Tower of London. What happened to the boys?

Before he died on April 9, 1483, King Edward IV named Edward V's uncle Richard, Duke of Gloucester, the Protector of the Kingdom until Edward V came of age.

That summer, the twelve-year-old king-in-waiting was housed in the Tower of London with his younger brother—another Richard, this one Duke of York. Next, the princes were declared illegitimate by an Act of Parliament named *Titulus Regius*, on the grounds that their father, Edward IV, had already been betrothed to another woman, Lady Eleanor Butler, when he married their mother, Elizabeth Woodville; this was taken as invalidating the marriage, and if the children were illegitimate, Edward V could not be crowned king. The Duke of Gloucester took the throne as King Richard III and was crowned on July 6 in a magnificent ceremony in Westminster Abbey.

That summer the young princes were seen playing and shooting arrows at straw bales in the gardens of the Tower, but afterward they were visible only very occasionally at the windows of the Garden Tower—and then disappeared altogether.

SMOTHERED IN THEIR BEDS?

The traditional view is based on the account given by English lawyer and statesman Sir Thomas More in his *History of King Richard the Third*, written long after the events concerned ca. 1512–19 and strongly slanted against Richard. More's book, which was a major influence on Shakespeare's play *Richard III*, and colors modern views of that king, reports that Richard ordered his servant Sir James Tyrell to do away with the princes: Tyrell hired two men, John Dighton and Miles Forrest, who crept into the royal bedchamber and suffocated them with pillows. Tyrell is said to have confessed to the murder before he was executed for treason in 1502; the treason was not the murder of the princes but supporting the claim to the throne of Edmund de la Pole, Duke of Suffolk, against that of the reigning king, Henry VII, in 1501.

Some historians think Henry Stafford, Duke of Buckingham, or King Henry VII might have murdered the princes. Henry VII married Elizabeth of York, the princes' older sister, in 1486, the year after he became king by defeating Richard III in the Battle of Bosworth Field: to wed her he had to repeal the *Titulus Regius* act that had declared her and them illegitimate and, therefore, he would have needed to eliminate them so they could not be rivals

Above: The Tower of London was the traditional place for royals to live while awaiting coronation —but Edward's coronation was delayed, first temporarily and then permanently.

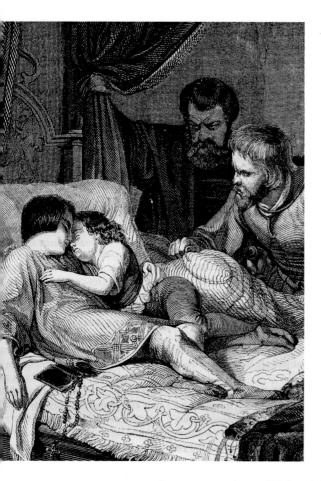

Above: If we are to believe in Thomas More's depiction of Richard III, then the king ordered the two princes to be murdered in their beds.

for the throne. Stafford was a descendant of Edward III and had his own claim to the throne, so might have been trying to clear his way to the crown. Aside from smothering, other proposed methods include poisoning and drowning in a butt of sweet "malmsey wine."

SAFETY IN EXILE?

Others think the princes were smuggled abroad to safety by men working on behalf of Richard III. Supporters of this theory argue that Richard wanted them gone, since they represented a threat to his power, and having got them safely away could not bring them back, even to quash rumors that he had killed them, because they would again become figureheads of opposition to his rule. In Henry VII's reign, two claimants to the throne, Lambert Simnel and Perkin Warbeck, both claimed to be the younger prince—Richard, Duke of York. (Simnel later changed his mind and said he was Edward Plantagenet, Earl of Warwick.) Some writers think Warbeck really was Richard and that this explains the ferocity of Henry VII's response to the Warbeck rebellion.

The consensus of many modern historians is that the princes were murdered, and on the orders of Richard III. Henry VII brought an act of attainder against his predecessor that, along with "unnatural, mischievous, and great perjuries, treasons, homicides, and murders," accused him of "shedding of infant's blood."

— STRANGE —
STORIES

Did seventeenth-century workmen dig up the bodies of the murdered princes? Sir Thomas More's account of the murder of the Princes in the Tower reports that the princes' bodies were buried at the foot of the stairs, "suitably deep in the ground under a great heap of stones." Almost 200 years later, in 1674, workmen digging at the Tower uncovered a wooden box 12 feet (3.6 meters) underground, containing what seemed to be the skeletons of two children. This matches More's account of the burial and seems to corroborate his main claim

Above: Modern historians have tried without success to convince the dean of Westminster Abbey to allow the bones to be exhumed so they can be DNA-tested.

that the princes were killed on Richard's orders by men working for Sir James Tyrell. Of course, this was long before modern DNA analysis was available, so no one could determine whether they were the bones of the princes, but everyone assumed they were. Charles II, the king at that time, had the bodies relocated to Westminster Abbey.

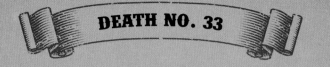

WAS THE CIA BEHIND THE DEATH OF MARILYN MONROE?

Date: August 5, 1962
Location: Brentwood, Los Angeles, California

The Hollywood actress and international sex symbol apparently committed suicide, but conspiracy theories have suggested she was murdered.

One of the most iconic figures of the twentieth century, Marilyn Monroe died a famous death—found naked in bed, with a telephone receiver in her hand, after apparently taking an overdose of barbiturates. She was only 36. The official verdict was probable suicide, but conspiracy theories of murder, perhaps involving the CIA, have swirled around the case for years.

Born Norma Jeane Mortenson in Los Angeles in 1926, Monroe was raised largely in an orphanage and a series of foster homes, and was working in a factory in 1944 when she was launched on a career as a pin-up model. She began in Hollywood with Twentieth Century Fox in 1946, changing her name to Marilyn Monroe, and

Right: By 1953, Monroe was playing a "dumb blonde" with great aplomb in a string of classic cult movies.

after successes in *All About Eve* and *Niagara* was a major star. In 1954, amid immense publicity, Monroe married an icon in baseball, star Joe DiMaggio, who had helped the New York Yankees win nine World Series in 1936–51. The marriage lasted only a year.

Then, unhappy at her treatment by Fox, Monroe tried to establish her own production company and build her career, studying acting at the celebrated Actors Studio in New York in 1955. Monroe won acclaim for her performances in *Bus Stop* (1956) and *Some Like it Hot* (1959), being awarded a Best Actress Golden Globe for the latter. By this time she had married celebrated playwright Arthur Miller. Her final film was the Western *The Misfits* in 1961, in a

part written by Miller, whom she had divorced in 1960, and starring with Clark Gable under the direction of John Huston.

By 1962 Monroe was often unwell and frequently absent from the set of the film she had been cast in, a comedy named *Something's Got to Give*, which was never finished. In May, she made it to New York, and at a gala performance in Madison Square Garden, gave her famous breathless rendition of "Happy Birthday, Mr. President" to President John F. Kennedy, with whom she was allegedly having an affair. The following month she was fired from the film.

Above: Marilyn with JFK (right) and Robert Kennedy (left) on the famous "Happy Birthday" night.

She was later rehired, but production never recommenced, and Monroe spent her last few months more or less as a recluse.

DEATH IN BRENTWOOD

In 1961 Monroe had moved back to Los Angeles, after spending around six years on the East Coast, and bought a house in the Brentwood area. It was here, at 12305 Fifth Helena Drive, that she died. She went to bed at around 8 p.m. on August 5. She received a telephone call from her friend, the actor Peter Lawford, who tried without success to get her to come out to a party; he said she sounded like she was heavily drugged and contacted his agent who tried unsuccessfully to reach her doctor. He did get through to her lawyer, Mickey Rudin, who reputedly called her housekeeper Eunice Murray to check on Monroe, and was told all was well.

The housekeeper, who was staying overnight, woke at around 3 a.m., sensing something was wrong. A light was on in Monroe's bedroom but the door was locked and Murray was unable to get a response. She called the star's psychiatrist, Ralph Greenson, who gained access via a window and found Monroe dead in bed. Her doctor, Hyman Engelberg, was called and arrived at about 3:50 a.m.

Empty pill bottles were found next to Monroe's bed and it was determined that she had died of acute barbiturate poisoning. She had died between 8:30 and 10:30 the previous night and because her doctors disclosed that she was subject to "severe fears and frequent depressions" and "abrupt and unpredictable" mood changes, and had made suicide attempts in the past, the LA County coroner ruled probable suicide. The possibility of accidental overdose was ruled out because experts reported Monroe's intake of barbiturates was way, way over the recommended dosage and had been ingested very quickly.

Below: Marilyn's room after her death: the star was found dead in bed—the mystery had begun.

Above: Had Monroe crossed paths with the Mob, and did she need to be silenced?

HUSH-UP?

A whole range of conspiracy theories arose in the years after Monroe's death. One, associated with anti-communist author Frank Capell, was that she was killed on the orders of Attorney General Robert Kennedy to hush up an affair they had been having; the theory argued that Kennedy was a communist sympathizer and the murder was part of an international communist conspiracy. Another version, proposed by journalist Anthony Scaduto, was that Monroe had a red diary containing confidential information about the Kennedys that went missing from her home.

Another theory, suggested by private detective and author Milo Speriglio, was that the Mafia or unions were responsible. Allegedly, Monroe's home had been wiretapped on the orders of union boss Jimmy Hoffa or of Sam Giancana, a Chicago mobster. In one theory, Giancana is supposed to have sent mobster hitmen to silence Monroe, who had been having an affair with one of Giancana's men, Johnny Roselli, and was threatening to speak out.

Another account, associated with Monroe biographer Anthony Summers, is that Robert Kennedy and Peter Lawford (Monroe's friend and Kennedy's brother-in-law) embarked on a campaign of encouraging the star's addiction to keep her quiet over the affair with Kennedy; she allegedly overdosed and died on the way to the hospital, but the death was staged as an at-home suicide to enable Robert Kennedy to get out of LA before the news broke. Another version, associated with another biographer, Donald Spoto, is that Monroe accidentally overdosed on drugs provided by Greenson and Engelberg and that her doctors covered it up as a suicide.

None of these theories has been proven. In the face of rumors that Monroe had been murdered, the LA County district attorney ordered an inquiry; it found no credible evidence to support this.

— STRANGE —
STORIES

Was the CIA involved in Monroe's death? This is another conspiracy theory of the star's death, proposed principally by British author Matthew Smith. This theory is that the CIA carried out the hit on Monroe because of her association with Robert Kennedy: they wanted to damage the Kennedys because they resented the way the Bay of Pigs Invasion in Cuba had been handled by President John F. Kennedy. An allied theory is that Monroe knew the truth about the Roswell UFO incident. The idea was that President Kennedy had told Monroe that he had seen extraterrestrial materials at the Roswell base and Monroe was threatening to hold a press conference on the matter. In the view of the CIA, the theory goes, she had to be silenced. Another outlandish claim was that Monroe's death was faked and she was committed to a mental institution in Canada by Greenson; she reputedly stayed alive there for 20 years and then was released.

Above: Maybe Monroe knew something of the Roswell incident, in which a UFO is said to have crashed in New Mexico and an alien given an autopsy.

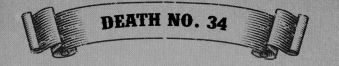

WAS THERE A COVER-UP OF THE KILLING OF SOCIALITE MARY PINCHOT MEYER?

Date: October 12, 1964
Location: Washington, D.C.

Some people allege CIA involvement in the shooting of artist Mary Pinchot Meyer, who had been a close friend of recently deceased President John F. Kennedy.

High-flying American artist and socialite Mary Pinchot Meyer was shot dead on a towpath in Washington, D.C., in October 1964. Her murder was never solved. Meyer had been married to CIA official Cord Meyer and, after her marriage ended, was romantically linked with President John F. Kennedy. She had often criticized the CIA and reportedly challenged the conclusions of the just-published Warren Commission report into the shooting of the president in November 1963. These and a number of other connections led some people to allege that the CIA was involved in her murder. Ray Crump, Jr., the man accused of killing her, was acquitted in July 1965. Some thought there was a high-level cover-up of what really happened.

Right: Cord and Mary Meyer were pacifists when they wed, but unbeknown to Mary, her husband then began to work for the CIA.

CLOSE CONNECTIONS

Born Mary Pinchot in New York City in 1920, the daughter of a wealthy lawyer and a journalist, and raised in Pennsylvania, she moved in rarefied social circles and met Kennedy as early as 1936. She and her husband, Cord Meyer, were committed pacifists and believers in global government when they wed in 1945, but Meyer was recruited to work secretly for the CIA from at least 1951 onward. In Washington, D.C., they were prominent members of the social elite in the prestigious Georgetown area, and Mary became close friends with the Kennedys; after her divorce in 1958, the CIA began to tap her phone.

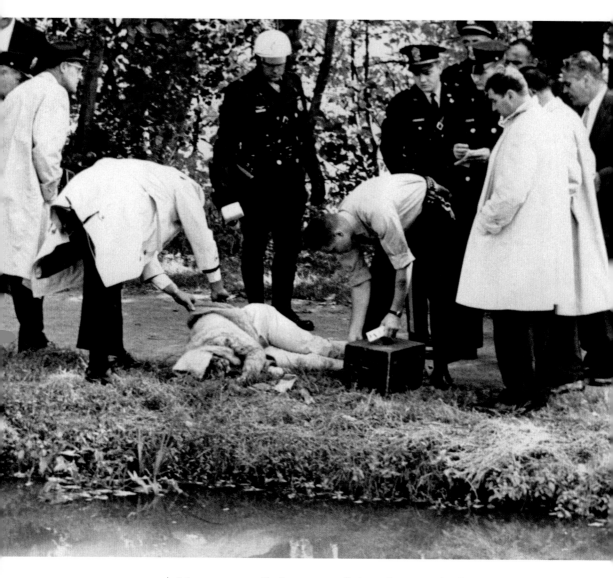

Above: Police examine the body of Mary, found on the towpath where she had so often gone for a walk.

Meyer reportedly began an affair with Kennedy shortly after he became president in 1961. A love letter from JFK to Meyer written a few weeks before his death in 1963 was sold at auction in 2016 for $88,970. He wrote: "Why don't you leave suburbia for once—come and see me—either here—or at the Cape next week or in Boston the 19th. I know it is unwise, irrational, and that you may hate it—on the other hand you may not—and I will love it."

On the day of her death, Meyer took a walk along the towpath of the Chesapeake and Ohio canal in Georgetown. She was shot twice, once in the temple and once in the back; later forensics found that the entry wounds were surrounded by "dark halos," indicating the shots were probably fired at point-blank range. A car mechanic named Henry Wiggins, working nearby, heard shots and, looking at the towpath, saw a black man standing over a white woman. Around 40 minutes later, a police detective arrested an African-American man, Ray Crump, who was walking nearby, on the basis of Wiggins' report—and the next day an army lieutenant, William Mitchell, reported having seen a black man trailing a white woman on the towpath and described clothing similar to what Crump had been wearing.

Crump was indicted. However, no gun was found and Crump was never linked in any way to a gun of the kind used in the murder; although Meyer's body had bled profusely from the head wound, no blood was found on Crump or his clothes. What's more, Crump's lawyer, Dovey Johnson Roundtree, was able to show at trial that witness reports described a man around 5 inches (13 cm) taller and 50 pounds (23 kg) heavier than Crump. As a result, Crump was acquitted. Roundtree later revealed that Crump had had a witness giving him an alibi at the time of the murder but that she disappeared before the trial.

Below: After her divorce in 1958, the CIA had begun to tap Mary's phone.

REVELATIONS

It later emerged, when army personnel records were released in 2015–16, that Lieutenant William Mitchell had links to the intelligence community. Another curious fact was that CIA official Wistar Janney apparently made phone calls to Meyer's brother-in-law, journalist Ben Bradlee, and her former husband, Cord Meyer, to inform them of her death in the afternoon of the day

Above: Mary was a close friend of JFK, and was present at his 46th birthday party on the presidential yacht *Sequoia*.

she was murdered—before the police had identified her body, suggesting that the agency somehow had advance knowledge of the murder or of the identity of the body.

A drama involving Meyer's diary came to light years later when Bradlee wrote in his 1995 memoir, *A Good Life*, that he had been alerted to the existence of the diary by Meyer's friend Anne Truitt. He wrote that he and his wife, Meyer's sister Antoinette ("Tony"), had gone to the artist's studio on the day after she was killed to retrieve the diary, which contained details of Meyer's affair with JFK, and encountered James Jesus Angleton, then chief of CIA Counterintelligence. They had found the diary and agreed on the need to keep its contents private. A press report suggested the diary was later burned.

Mary Pinchot Meyer's death was never fully explained. Her former husband, writing an autobiography in 1982, dismissed what he called "journalistic speculation" about the involvement of intelligence agencies and accepted the police line that the attack was sexually motivated. There are many curious elements that continue to feed speculation about a high-level cover-up surrounding the death of this very well-connected woman and the events of October 1964.

— STRANGE — STORIES

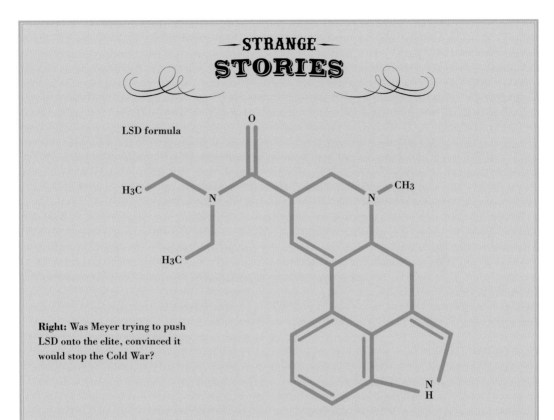

LSD formula

Right: Was Meyer trying to push LSD onto the elite, convinced it would stop the Cold War?

Controversial psychologist Timothy Leary, the one-time Harvard professor who advocated experimenting with psychedelic drugs, made the remarkable claim that in 1962 Meyer was engaged in trying to promote peace and counter the threat of the Cold War by convincing powerful members of the establishment to take mind-altering drugs. The idea was that they would gain new insight and be convinced to avert conflict. Meyer herself took LSD and was connected to Leary, but there is no evidence that she convinced JFK to try it. However, Leary did claim, in his 1983 autobiography, *Flashbacks*, that she contacted him after JFK's assassination. She allegedly said of JFK, "they couldn't control him anymore. He was changing too fast." She told Leary she was fearful for their safety: "I'm afraid. Be careful."

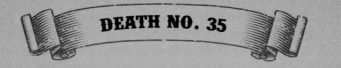

DID BRUCE LEE DIE AS THE RESULT OF A *DIM MAK* DEATH STRIKE?

Date: July 20, 1973
Location: Hong Kong

Kung fu superstar Bruce Lee officially died because of an allergic reaction to a painkiller, but conspiracy theories were soon circulating about his death at the age of just 32.

Kung fu teacher-turned-actor Bruce Lee became an international movie star and pop-culture sensation in martial arts movies of the 1970s. He died in puzzling circumstances in Hong Kong while working on the movie *Game of Death*, and rumors soon sprung up around the event.

Born in San Francisco and raised in Hong Kong, Lee first appeared in movies as a baby in the 1941 film *Golden Gate Girl*. He was the son of celebrated Cantonese opera star Lee Hoi-chuen. In Hong Kong Lee learned kung fu and took dance lessons and—always a good mover—won the 1958 Hong Kong cha-cha contest before moving back to the US, aged 18.

UNIQUE STYLE

In California Lee developed his own method of martial arts, *Jeet Kune Do*, which incorporated boxing and fencing with philosophy and more traditional martial arts moves. After a stint appearing in the TV show *The Green Hornet* in 1966–67 he taught his *Jeet Kune Do* method to Hollywood stars including James Coburn and Steve McQueen. Lee appeared in the 1969 movie *Marlowe* and did fight choreography in a few films, but moved back to Hong Kong in 1971. There, he became a star.

His movies *The Big Boss* and *Fist of Fury* in 1971–72 smashed box office records in Asia and *Way of the Dragon* (1972, with Chuck Norris) built on this triumph. *Enter the Dragon* (1973) was to make him a global star—but this movie was released after he died.

MOVIE OF DEATH

In 1973 Lee was in Hong Kong planning *Game of Death* with producer Raymond Chow and actress Betty Ting Pei. When Lee developed a severe headache, Ting gave him a painkiller. Lee went for a rest but Chow was later unable to wake him up; a doctor and then an ambulance were called, but Lee was dead by the time he reached the hospital.

An autopsy determined that Lee's brain had swelled as part of an allergic reaction to a tranquilizer named meprobamate, one of the ingredients in the painkiller he had

Below: The title of Lee's planned feature film, *Game of Death*, proved to be eerily prophetic.

Long live the King!

SPECIAL GUEST APPEARANCE OF—
KAREEM
ABDUL
JABBAR

Goodbye,
BRUCE LEE
HIS LAST GAME OF DEATH

been given, and the official ruling was "death by misadventure." Some sources suggest the death was associated with Lee consuming hashish to calm his nerves; cannabis was found in his stomach and while some medical experts said this could not have contributed to the seizure, others said it could.

Above: Reportedly, Lee chewed hashish and ate "hash brownies" (cakes containing cannabis) to steady his nerves.

Some suggested Lee had been assassinated by Chinese Triad gangs or that he was the victim of a *dim mak* (death strike). He had established his own film production company before making *Way of the Dragon* and the theory goes that he fell foul of the Triads by refusing them a role in this and a share in the profits. The *dim mak* strike is said to disrupt the natural flow of energy around the body; with expert insight a practitioner knows which spot on the body to hit to cause fatal bodily disruption—and this can be delayed, apparently, so that the effects are not felt until days or weeks later. Was Lee drawn into a fight on a movie set by a kung fu adept who delivered the fatal blow weeks prior to his death?

Other explanations were that Lee died because the painkiller reacted with the muscle relaxant he had been taking since 1968 to ease back pain, or that he had been taking too much cortisone, again, to ease his back pain.

— STRANGE —
STORIES

Above: Side by side in death, father and son died in tragically similar circumstances.

Lee's son Brandon also died at a young age and in extraordinary circumstances, fueling conspiracy theories that a curse had been placed on the family. Although his father had died when he was aged eight, Brandon had followed him into the movie business. He picked up TV and movie roles from 1985 onward, including *Rapid Fire*, his first starring role, in 1992. Then he was shot in an accident involving a prop gun on set while filming comic book movie *The Crow* in North Carolina, on March 30, 1993. Brandon was shot in the abdomen and rushed to a hospital where, despite six hours of surgery, he died. He was only 28.

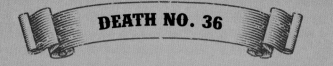

WAS THERE A CONSPIRACY BEHIND THE DEATH OF POPE JOHN PAUL I?

Date: September 28–29, 1978
Location: Vatican City, Italy

Conspiracy theories were soon circulating about the sudden death of John Paul I—only 33 days after his election as Pope.

The election of Cardinal Albino Luciani as Pope on August 26, 1978, was unexpected—and, according to some, not well received in all quarters of the Roman Catholic Church. This—together with the fact that he died so soon after his election, and that there were inconsistencies in initial reports about his death—fueled the conspiracy theories.

Nicknamed *il Papa del Sorriso* ("the Smiling Pope"), John Paul I was the first pope for many centuries to refuse to have a grand papal coronation, preferring to be invested with an archbishop's pallium rather than to be crowned. He seemed to be determined to do away with the traditional formality of his office and make the Pope a more "human" figure.

COURTING CONTROVERSY

Church authorities may not have liked this, and might also have been concerned over John Paul's ideas about contraception, banned for Roman Catholics under Pope Paul VI's encyclical *Humanae vitae*. In 1968, when he was Bishop of Vittorio Veneto, Luciani had recommended to Paul VI that the contraceptive pill be permitted for members of the Church.

Luciani's background was pastoral—in church work. He had not served, though, as a papal diplomat or on the Roman Curia, the Roman Catholic Church's central body of government. Some said that senior church figures did not respect his intellect. One unidentified cardinal is said to have sneered, "They have elected Peter Sellers," a reference to the British actor internationally famous above all for his performances as the incompetent yet bafflingly successful French policeman Inspector Clouseau in the *Pink Panther* series of movies.

John Paul I died from an apparent heart attack on the night of September 28–29, 1978. He went to bed on the 28th at about 9 p.m., after dining in his Vatican apartment with his secretaries Father Diego Lorenzi and Father John Magee. Early the next morning, he was discovered dead in his bed.

There were various inconsistencies in the facts given at the time. In addition, the authorities did not conduct an autopsy. When this issue was questioned, the Vatican said that autopsies were not held in the case of popes, although one had been conducted in the case of Pope Clement XIV (1769–74).

Below: "The Smiling Pope" was known for his good humor and personal warmth.

Above: Smiling in death as well as in life, John Paul I was laid to rest, apparently having died from a heart attack.

THE OFFICIAL ACCOUNTS

The book *Pope Luciani: Chronicle of a Death*, published in 2017 and written by Vatican journalist Stefania Falasca, relied on the following account. Sister Vincenza Taffarel left John Paul I his coffee in the sacristy of his chapel as usual at about 5:15 a.m., and then 10 minutes later, noticing he had not touched it, went into his room. She was shocked, and summoned Sister Margherita Marin, who also entered the room. They found him seated in bed in his pajamas, with a slight smile on his face and his glasses on his nose, his reading light still on and typewritten papers in his hands. Sister Margherita touched his hands and noticed how cold they were, and how dark his nails were. (Earlier accounts from the Vatican suggested that his male secretaries and not the nuns found him. There were also inconsistencies in timings.)

After they had raised the alarm, the deputy head of the Vatican's health service, Dr. Renato Buzzonetti, examined the body and said that the Pope had suffered a heart attack the previous night at about 11 p.m.

Falasca's book also revealed that the Pope had suffered from severe chest pain while praying vespers with Father Magee the night before he died. The Pope turned down an offer to contact his doctor, Buzzonetti, and the pain went away. In a foreword to the book, senior churchman Secretary of State Cardinal Pietro Parolin said that John Paul had treated heart trouble with anticoagulant drugs earlier in life, while Patriach of Venice in 1975. Falasca, who also has an official Vatican position—vice-postulator, dedicated to gathering materials supporting the Pope's elevation to sainthood—declared that John Paul I did indeed die of a heart attack.

— STRANGE —
STORIES

One theory favored by those arguing that Pope John Paul I was killed is that he was about to expose corruption in the Vatican Bank that linked it to the Mafia. Part of this theory is the contention that the papers found in the Pope's hand listed names of senior churchmen who were Freemasons, and who were connected to financial shenanigans used to launder Mafia drug profits. These claims have been published, notably in the 1984 book *In God's Name* by David Yallop, but never proven. Another theory is that the Pope was terminated to prevent his demoting a cadre of very powerful members of the Church's highest ranks. A third theory is that John Paul I was preparing to reintroduce the traditionalist Tridentine Mass, celebrated in Latin, which had been largely succeeded by the Mass of Paul VI, introduced by that pope in 1969. It is speculated that he was killed to prevent his bringing back the Tridentine Mass.

Right: Was John Paul about to name and shame prominent figures in the Church as Freemasons, which is forbidden for Roman Catholics?

THEY WERE ALL LOST... GROUP TRAGEDIES

Sometimes, entire groups disappear from the pages of history, as if at a stroke. Perhaps subsequent records of the group have been destroyed, or its members were all lost at once in a tragic event. Either might have been the case with the celebrated IX Legio Hispana (the "Spanish Legion") of the Roman Army, which was last recorded at the Roman colonia of Eboracum (modern York, in northern England) and, thereafter, apparently disappeared. One theory is that they were wiped out in an attack by the widely feared Brigantes tribe of what is now northern England; another that they were transferred to another country and are simply lost to the historical record.

Close to 1,400 years later, Italian explorer John Cabot was in the pay of England's King Henry VII when he and his entire crew disappeared on a voyage seeking to find an eastern route from Europe to Asia in 1498. Some think they were lost at sea, but others believe the trip was a success and that Cabot returned to England, where he died later, perhaps from the plague. Closer to the modern era, intrepid German-born explorer Ludwig Leichhardt and seven members of his team disappeared in the Australian Outback. Their bodies have never been discovered and debates continue as to how far they got, whether they were killed by Indigenous Australians, whether they ran out of supplies and died of starvation, or whether they "went native." Subsequent expeditions have failed to turn up much evidence of the group.

Left: Explorer Ludwig Leichhardt finds a body from a lost expedition in the inhospitable Outback, before becoming lost himself.

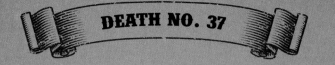

WHO WIPED OUT THE FAMOUS IX SPANISH LEGION?

Date: ca. 120 CE
Location: Scotland or Northern England

The disappearance of the Ninth Legion has never been fully explained, and there are several theories about what happened to these brave and disciplined Roman men of war.

The Roman army's famous Legio IX Hispana disappeared from history in around 120 CE. Some think its soldiers were annihilated in battle by British or Caledonian (Scottish) tribes, others that they were transferred abroad and met their end there—perhaps in Armenia.

The Ninth Legion had a long and famous history. It fought as early as 90 BCE in the "Social War," the fight against the *socii*—the Roman city-state's allies in Italy who had risen in revolt. After that, the soldiers of the Ninth served with great distinction for Roman General Julius Caesar in Gaul (France) and on his campaigns against his rival Pompey. Caesar disbanded the group

Above: Legions formed the Roman army's elite heavy infantry, and were recruited exclusively from Roman citizens.

following his final victory ca. 45 BCE, but ca. 30 BCE the legion was reconstituted as part of the establishment of the Imperial Army under Emperor Augustus and sent to Hispania (Spain)— from which it took its name.

The Ninth probably took part in the conquest of Britain led by Aulus Plautius in 43 CE. We know that in 50 CE they were one of two legions who defeated British resistance leader Caratacus, chief of the Catuvellauni tribe, in the celebrated Battle of Caer Caradoc—probably in Herefordshire or Shropshire, UK. They also built a fort at Lindum Colonia (now Lincoln), and crushed the first rebellion of Venutius of the Brigantes tribe while Aulus Didius Gallus was governor (52–57 CE). They were part of the Roman army crushed and humiliated at Camulodunum (Colchester) during the rebellion of Boudicca in 61 CE. So many legionaries were killed in this encounter that major reinforcement from Germany was necessary.

In 82–83 CE they took part in the invasion of Caledonia led by Agricola, and survived a night attack on their makeshift fort somewhere north of the River Forth, as described by the Roman historian Tacitus. They fought in the Roman victory at the Battle of Mons Graupius (the exact location of which is still disputed).

LAST TRACES

The last reference in the historical record in Britain is an inscription from 108 CE recording the role of the Ninth in the rebuilding of the fortress at Eboracum (York). After that, recently discovered inscriptions from ca. 104–120 CE indicate that the legion—or a detachment from it—was at Noviomagus Batavorum (Nijmegen), a fortress on the Rhine in the Netherlands, and at Aachen, Germany.

A traditional theory, put forward by nineteenth-century German classicist Theodor Mommsen before the discovery of the Nijmegen fragments, is that the legion was wiped out by the Brigantes tribe sometime after 108 CE. When Emperor Hadrian came to Britain ca. 122 CE, he embarked on building Hadrian's Wall across 73 miles (118 kilometers) of northern England, to control incursions by local tribes, and it's possible that he was prompted to do this by a major attack of the kind suggested by Mommsen. A new legion, the Sixth, came with Hadrian and settled at York—suggesting manpower was needed to replace the men of the Ninth.

Above: The celebrated Hadrian's Wall was built, according to the third-century Augustan History, because "the Britons could not be kept under Roman control."

Another theory suggests a similar fate for the legion, but in Scotland. This was dramatized in the celebrated 1954 children's novel *The Eagle of the Ninth* by British novelist Rosemary Sutcliff. In this book, the legion goes north to fight the Scots and suffers a calamitous defeat there that wipes them out; a movie adaptation, *The Eagle*, was released in 2011, directed by Kevin Macdonald and starring Channing Tatum and Jamie Bell.

Other historians argue that the Ninth Legion was transferred abroad and either eliminated or disbanded there. One theory (see box, page 203) suggests they were wiped out in Judaea, another

Below: Calgacus, Caledonian chief of the tribes of northern Britain, addresses his army before facing the Romans—including the Ninth Legion—under Agricola at the Battle of Mons Graupius.

argues that the Ninth fought and were destroyed in Marcus Aurelius's campaigns against the Parthians ca. 161: the Greco-Roman historian Cassius Dio records that a Roman legion was annihilated in a battle against a Parthian force led by their general Chosroes, after which Marcus Sedatius Severianus, governor of the Roman province of Cappadocia (now central/eastern Turkey), took his own life. However, there is no other evidence of the Ninth Legion having been in this part of the world, and as the historical record is silent about the Ninth after ca. 120 at the latest, where was it and what was it doing for the 40 years until 161 CE?

— STRANGE —
STORIES

Some argue that the great massacre that destroyed the Ninth Legion was not in the British Isles but Judaea. One theory holds that the redoubtable soldiers of the Ninth were drafted in to help fight the Second Jewish Revolt in 132–136 CE. This uprising was provoked by the Romans building a shrine to Jupiter on Temple Mount in Jerusalem. Led by Simon bar Kokhba, the rebels briefly established an independent Jewish state, but were finally crushed by the imperial army. Emperor Hadrian summoned one of his leading generals, Sextus Julius Severus, from Britain, and he brought three legions, possibly including the Ninth, with him. He eventually crushed the uprising, but some say the Ninth was swept away—alongside another legion, XXII Deiotariana, that disappears from the historical record at about this time—in a heavy defeat in the course of this bloody struggle.

Above: Was this flag flying in Jerusalem, where the Ninth may have been crushing an uprising?

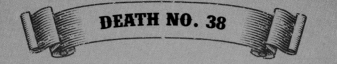

WHAT BECAME OF JOHN CABOT AND HIS FLEET?

Date: ca. 1498–1501
Location: Atlantic Ocean?

The traditional view is that the Italian explorer and his men drowned on a voyage paid for by Henry VII of England, but could they have returned to England after all?

Venetian navigator John Cabot embarked from Bristol with five ships in May 1498, seeking an eastern sea route to Asia. At least one ship was damaged and landed in Ireland, and it is generally assumed that the remainder of the fleet was lost at sea. However, some historians argue that Cabot's trip was a success, and he returned to England in 1500 after exploring the east coast of North America, maybe making it as far south as the Caribbean. If he did ever return to Bristol, his death seems to have come in an outbreak of plague shortly after.

Born Giovanni Caboto in Genoa ca. 1450, Cabot traded along the Mediterranean for many years before moving to England, where he settled in Bristol. He made a successful and well-documented voyage in 1497 before the mysterious voyage the following year.

THE 1497 VOYAGE

On May 2, 1497, with the backing of King Henry VII, Cabot sailed aboard the ship *Matthew* with 18 men. The intention was to make landfall in "Asia." They did find land—and went ashore somewhere in North America, probably in Newfoundland or on Cape Breton Island in Nova Scotia, although some historians suggest they may have hit what is now Labrador in Canada or Maine in the United States. Cabot thought it was Asia; he called it "New-found-land." (The official landing point, designated by Canada in 1997 as part of the celebration of the 500th anniversary of Cabot's voyage, is Cape Bonavista in Newfoundland.) He and his men went ashore, took on fresh water, and saw evidence of human life—a wooden tool, the remains of a fire, nets, and a manmade trail. They claimed the land for Henry VII and England, also raising the papal and Venetian banners.

Cabot's fleet explored the coast and its waters. He named the following features: Cape Discovery (probably Cape North), the island of St. John (St. Paul Island), St. George's Cape (Cape Ray),

Below: The Italian explorer and his expedition land on the shore of Labrador in 1497.

the Trinity Islands (St. Pierre and Miquelon), and England's Cape (Cape Race). He returned to Bristol on August 6 to great acclaim. Traveling to London, he received a reward of £10 (around two years' craftsman's wages at the time), was honored everywhere he went, and was awarded a substantial pension.

THE FINAL VOYAGE

In May 1498 one of Cabot's five ships was fitted and supplied by the king. The ships held various items for trade, including cloth, lace, and other merchandise. The aim was to find Japan. One of the ships landed in Ireland after being damaged in a storm, and the traditional view is that the main fleet was lost at sea. Cabot's death was assumed to have been a watery one somewhere in the Atlantic Ocean. This is what Italian humanist scholar Polydore Vergil determined in his *Anglica Historia* of ca. 1512. He wrote that the only lands this explorer found were on the bottom of the ocean, but many historians argue that it is almost unheard of for an entire fleet to go missing, and that while some ships may have been sunk, others probably survived and landed in North America.

Below: It is fitting that there are statues of Cabot at both Cape Bonavista (his official landing point), and Bristol (below), his departure point—and intended return point.

An associated claim is that a group of Augustinian friars from Milan, led by Father Giovanni Antonio de Carbonarius, was on board a ship named *Dominus Nobiscum* ("The Lord Be With Us"), as part of Cabot's fleet, and after the ships reached North America, settled there to found a mission in Newfoundland—North America's first Christian settlement—probably at Carbonear on the Avalon Peninsula. This claim is being investigated in an archaeological dig at Carbonear by the Memorial University of Newfoundland.

― STRANGE ―
STORIES

Some historians think Cabot and his men may have landed in North America and never returned, but another theory is that they returned safely to England. British historian Alwyn Ruddock suggested the fleet returned to England in spring 1500, her argument partly based on the Spanish cartographer Juan de la Cosa's map of the world, which reputedly showed areas of the coast of North America "discovered by the English" in 1497–1500. One of the men known to have sailed with Cabot in 1498, a London merchant named Lancelot Thirkill, was in London on June 6, 1501, when he made a bond to which a royal document of 1506 refers. In addition, Cabot's annual £20 pension was paid in the years 1497–98 and 1498–99. Is this proof that he returned, or does it merely reflect the fact that one of the explorer's nearest and dearest, likely his wife, Mattea, was drawing out the money on his behalf?

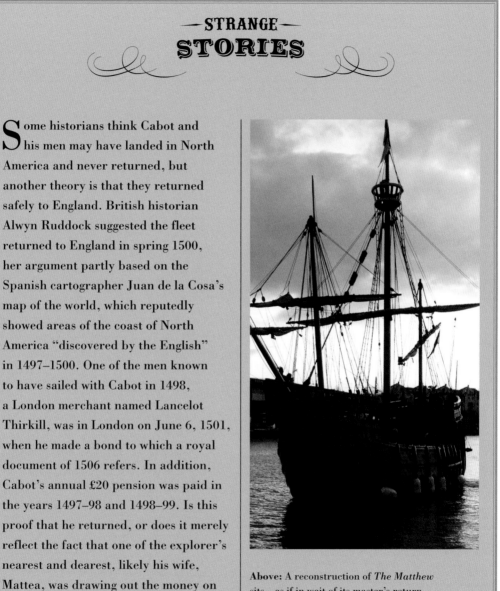

Above: A reconstruction of *The Matthew* sits—as if in wait of its master's return— on the waters of Bristol harbor.

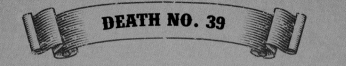

WERE LUDWIG LEICHHARDT AND HIS MEN LOST IN THE OUTBACK?

Date: April 3, 1848
Location: Darling Downs, Australia

The German explorer and his seven-man team disappeared on a trip into the interior of Australia. Did they starve to death or were they killed by indigenous Australians?

Ludwig Leichhardt and his intrepid team went missing in April 1848 while attempting a daring east to west crossing of Australia. They were last seen on April 3, 1848, at Cogoon on the Darling Downs in southern Queensland. A series of search expeditions failed to determine what happened to them, although there are several tantalizing pieces of evidence.

German-born Leichhardt did widespread fieldwork in Europe before arriving in Sydney in 1842, determined to explore the inhospitable Australian interior. He carried out a successful trip from Darling Downs to Port Essington in the Northern Territory, a distance of 3,000 miles (4,800 kilometers). The trip took so

Left: Leichhardt published a journal of his successful—but lengthy—1844–45 trip and won prizes from the Paris Geographical Society and the Royal Geographical Society, London.

long—from August 1844 to December 1845—that many thought the party had been lost or killed, and when they made it back to civilization, in Sydney, on March 25, 1846, they were greeted as heroes.

After the forced abandoning of a second trip due to famine, malaria, and heavy rains, Leichhardt began his final trip in Queensland, March 1848, aiming to travel right across the country and reach Perth. He had with him four fellow-Europeans—Adolph Classen, Thomas Hands, Arthur Hentig, and Donald Stuart—and two indigenous guides, Wommai and Billy Bombat. They had 7 horses, 50 bullocks, and 20 mules.

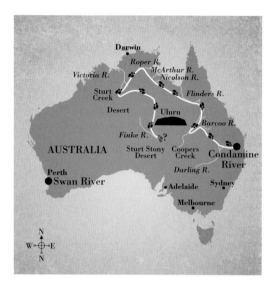

Above: Instead of finding Perth, Leichhardt and his team may have found themselves following the route marked on the map above, trekking deep into Australia's expansive interior.

The trip was expected to take two years, and after three years with no word from the group, people had to accept that they had perished.

FRAGMENTARY EVIDENCE

Various search parties have turned up fragmentary clues. In 1852 a party found a tree marked "L" and "XVA"; a second party found two more trees marked "L" in 1858. Two further marked trees were found by the Flinders River by another explorer in 1864. Yet another expedition was sent out in 1869, in response to reports that there was a place in Western Australia where the remains of white men and their animals who had been attacked by indigenous Australians could be seen; the party found nothing.

In 1896 David Carnegie's expedition into the Gibson and Great Sandy deserts met some Indigenous Australians who had an iron tent peg, part of an iron fitting from a saddle, and a section of tin matchbox, and speculated that these might have been Leichhardt's possessions. There were reports of cave paintings depicting white men and an animal and even of white men seen living among Indigenous people—survivors gone native?

Probably the best piece of evidence is a small brass plate marked "Ludwig Leichhardt 1848," found in 1900 by a stockman just across the border from the Northern Territory into Western Australia, between the Tanami Desert and the Great Sandy Desert. He found the plate attached to part of a shotgun that was tied to a tree marked with an "L." This find suggests that Leichhardt and his men traveled more than two-thirds of the way across the interior of the great Australian continent before perishing.

— STRANGE —
STORIES

One striking theory is that Leichhardt and his party were killed by indigenous Australians—Aboriginals— in the area of Wallumbilla, Queensland. The evidence comes in a letter discovered in 2003 in the New South Wales State Library: dated April 2, 1874, it had been sent to a clergyman named William Branwhite Clarke by a station owner from Darling Downs, W.D. Gordon, who had encountered Leichhardt and his party shortly before they disappeared. Gordon later made friends with members of the Wallumbilla tribe in Queensland, and they told him of a tribal legend that many years earlier a group of Indigenous people had surrounded and killed a white man and a group of bullocks and mules on the Maranoa River in the basin of the Murray and Darling Rivers. If this is true, the Wallumbilla tribe must have traded the materials with other groups— for the metal plate and rifle butt turned

Above: Did the expedition perish at the hands of a Queensland tribe? If so, their progress was almost negligible, given the enormity of the task, ending in the state in which they started.

up 2,500 miles (4,000 kilometers) away. It would also mean that Leichhardt and his men made far less progress in their crossing of Australia than previously thought.

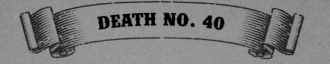

WHAT HAPPENED TO ROALD AMUNDSEN AND HIS CREW?

Date: June 18, 1928
Location: Barents Sea, Arctic

Amundsen and a crew of five disappeared while searching for fellow explorer Umberto Nobile in the Arctic.

Intrepid Norwegian explorer Roald Amundsen—the man who pipped Englishman Captain Robert Scott in the race to the South Pole in 1911–12—died as he loved to live, taking on the elements at the ends of the earth. He was leading a rescue mission to save Umberto Nobile, an Italian adventurer with whom he had flown across the North Pole in 1926 in Nobile's airship *Norge*. In 1928 a different Nobile airship, *Italia*, had crashed when returning from a new mission, and Amundsen's team set out in a French Latham 47 flying boat to search for him. The Norwegian rescue mission itself went missing on June 18, 1928, and although parts of their flying boat have been found, indicating that it made a forced landing, the explorers' bodies have never been recovered.

A LIFE OF ADVENTURES

Amundsen was a lifelong explorer. In his twenties he took part in the first expedition to winter in the Antarctic, aboard a Belgian ship called the RV *Belgica*, in 1897–99. Then in 1903–06, aboard the 45-tonne *Gjøa*, he led the first transit through the Northwest Passage that links the Atlantic and Pacific Oceans. On his next trip, his team was the first to reach the South Pole, arriving on December 14, 1911, 34 days before the British team led by Captain Robert Scott made it there.

Right: Amundsen may have been an intrepid explorer, but he was one who, in the attempt to rescue fellow explorers, needed rescuing himself.

From 1918 to 1925, Amundsen tried to reach the North Pole on his ship the *Maud*, but gave that up in favor of an airborne attempt. On May 11–13, 1926, he flew across the North Pole in the airship *Norge*, in a team of 16 including Lincoln Ellsworth and Umberto Nobile. In doing so, Amundsen became the first person to have reached both South and North Poles. In addition, his team may have been the first to reach the North Pole: three previous attempts had all claimed to have done this, but there are doubts over every claim—those of American explorers Frederick Cook in 1908, Robert Peary in 1909, and Richard E. Byrd earlier in 1926.

In 1928 Nobile's *Italia* airship was exploring the Arctic from a base on Spitsbergen, Norway. On May 25, while returning from the North Pole, the ship crashed around 75 miles (120 kilometers) northeast of the Norwegian archipelago of Svalbard. Its radio operator, Giuseppe Biagi, began sending out the emergency SOS signal, indicating the crew were in dire trouble. Amundsen's doomed rescue flight was one of several attempts to save the crash survivors. In the end, there were eight survivors, including Nobile. Amundsen and his rescue crew were not among them.

DOOMED RESCUE MISSION

Amundsen took off from Tromsø, Norway, on June 18 in a twin-engine Latham 47 flying boat, with Norwegian aviation pioneer Leif Dietrichson, Frenchman René Guilbaud, and three other French fliers. Their last radio message came through at 6 p.m. Historians believe that the plane had to make an emergency landing in the Barents Sea in heavy fog.

On the basis of where the last radio message came from, experts believe the flying boat came down near Bjørnøya (Bear Island), the farthest south of the islands of the Svalbard archipelago. A second rescue mission was launched to save the Amundsen rescue mission, or at least find out what had happened to it. After much fruitless searching, this was abandoned in September 1928.

Right: Captain Amundsen (left), and fellow polar explorer Lincoln Ellsworth, watching the arrival of the *Norge* after its flight from Leningrad to Spitsbergen, for the purpose of taking them across the North Pole to Alaska.

In the 1930s a fisherman found a wing float and a gasoline tank from the flying boat in the sea off Tromsø. There is evidence that there was at least one survivor of the landing, because there are marks on the fuel tank made by a hammer and a knife, indicating that someone was trying to use it as a flotation device.

Above: The Latham 47 in Tromsø, shortly before Amundsen took off in search of Umberto Nobile, never to be seen again.

The bodies of the intrepid crew were never found and their ultimate fate remains a mystery. How many survived? Did they manage to reach land or an ice floe? If they survived, how long did they endure? A mysterious disappearance in the frozen wastes of the Arctic was a fitting end for possibly the greatest of all polar explorers.

— STRANGE —
STORIES

The disappearance of this great polar adventurer has fascinated historians for 90 years. The Norwegian navy launched an attempt to find wreckage of the Latham 47 flying boat in the Barents Sea in 2009, using an unmanned submarine, the *HUGIN 1000*, which traveled across the seafloor looking for wreckage. On board the Norwegian ship, the *Tyr*, was a direct descendant of Amundsen, Nikolay Jacobsen. The investigative mission followed the route taken by the 1930s fisherman who caught Amundsen's

Above: To this day, none of the wreckage has been found in the Barents Sea, despite a concerted—and documented—effort in 2009.

wing float. They searched an area of the seafloor measuring 36 square nautical miles (123 sq kilometers) situated around 20 miles (32 kilometers) to the northwest of Bear Island—but without luck. The mission was filmed for a 2010 documentary, directed by Rudolph Herzog, *Amundsen: Lost in the Arctic.*

FURTHER READING

Bierman, John. *Righteous Gentile: The Story of Raoul Wallenberg, Missing Hero of the Holocaust*. Harmondsworth, Middlesex: Penguin, 1995.

Carlberg, Ingrid & Annan, & Kofi Atta. *Raoul Wallenberg: The Heroic Life and Mysterious Disappearance of the Man Who Saved Thousands of Hungarian Jews from the Holocaust*. London: MacLehose Press, Quercus, 2016.

Cathcart, Brian. *Jill Dando: Her Life and Death*. Harmondsworth, Middlesex: Penguin, 2001.

Danisi, Thomas C. & Jackson, John C. *Meriwether Lewis*. Amherst, New York: Prometheus Books, 2009.

Finstad, Suzanne. *Natasha: The Biography of Natalie Wood*. New York City: Arrow, 2002.

Florescu, Radu R. & McNally, Raymond T. *Dracula, Prince of Many Faces: His Life and His Times*. Boston, Massachusetts: Little, Brown, 2005.

Fox, E. T. *King of the Pirates: The Swashbuckling Life of Henry Every*. Stroud, Gloucestershire: The History Press, 2008.

Frame, Tom. *The Life and Death of Harold Holt*. Crows Nest, Australia: Allen & Unwin, 2005.

Gillies, Midge. *Amy Johnson: Queen of the Air*. London: Phoenix, 2004.

Gillingham, John. *William II: The Red King*. London: Allen Lane, 2015.

Hearst, Patricia & Biddle, Cordelia Frances. *Murder at San Simeon*. New York City: Scribner, 2012.

Hemmleb, Jochen & Johnson, Larry A. *Ghosts of Everest: The Authorised Story of the Search for Mallory and Irvine*. Basingstoke: Macmillan, 1999.

Lawrence, Sharon. *Jimi Hendrix: The Man, the Magic, the Truth*. London: Pan, 2006.

Nicol, Donald M. *The Immortal Emperor: The Life and Legend of Constantine Palaiologos, Last Emperor of the Romans.* Cambridge: Cambridge University Press, 2010.

Phillips, Seymour. *Edward II (The English Monarchs Series).* New Haven, Connecticut: Yale University Press, 2011.

Poe, Edgar Allen. *The Mystery of Marie Rogêt.* Seattle, Washington: CreateSpace Independent Publishing Platform, 2014.

Polly, Matthew. *Bruce Lee: A Life.* New York City: Simon & Schuster, 2018.

Spoto, Donald. *Marilyn Monroe: The Biography.* New York City: Arrow, 1994.

Spragg, Dennis M. *Glenn Miller Declassified.* Lincoln, Nebraska: Potomac Books, 2017.

Taves, Brian. *Thomas Ince: Hollywood's Independent Pioneer.* Lexington, Kentucky: University Press of Kentucky, 2012.

Thompson, Hunter S. *Fear and Loathing in Las Vegas.* New York City: Harper Perennial, 2005.

Tyldesley, Joyce. *Nefertiti's Face: Creation of an Icon.* London: Profile Books, 2015.

Weir, Alison. *Mary Queen of Scots: And the Murder of Lord Darnley.* New York City: Vintage, 2008.

Weir, Alison. *Richard III and the Princes in the Tower.* New York City: Vintage, 2014.

Wilkes, Roger. *Wallace: The Final Verdict.* London: The Bodley Head, 1984.

Web

Schiff, Stacy. "Saint-Exupéry Lands at Last." *The New York Times*, April 11, 2004. www.nytimes.com/2004/04/11/opinion/saint-exupery-lands-at-last.html

Grann, David. "The Lost City of Z." *New Yorker*, September 19, 2005. paidpost.newyorker.com/lostcityofz/

The Great Web of Percy Harrison Fawcett. www.phfawcettsweb.org/stefan.htm

"Fiancee Predicts Suicide of Actor George Reeves." California Digital Newspaper Collection. cdnc.ucr.edu/cgi-bin/cdnc?a=d&d=DS19590616.2.23

Bristol, John Cabot and the Discovery of The Americas. matthew.co.uk/1497-voyage

Dr. Miles Russell. "The Roman Ninth Legion's Mysterious Loss." www.bbc.co.uk/news/magazine-12752497

INDEX

IMAGE CREDITS